WORKING WITH WOOD

TIME LIFE
BOOKS

This volume is part of a series offering home
owners detailed instructions on repairs,
construction and improvements which they can
undertake themselves.

HOME REPAIR
AND IMPROVEMENT

WORKING WITH WOOD

BY THE EDITORS OF
TIME-LIFE BOOKS

TIME-LIFE BOOKS
AMSTERDAM

TIME-LIFE BOOKS

EUROPEAN EDITOR: Kit van Tulleken
Design Director: Ed Skyner
Photography Director: Pamela Marke
Chief of Research: Vanessa Kramer
Chief Sub-Editor: Ilse Gray

HOME REPAIR AND IMPROVEMENT

EDITORIAL STAFF FOR WORKING WITH WOOD
Editor: William Frankel
Designer: Kenneth E. Hancock
Chief Researcher: Phyllis K. Wise
Picture Editor: Adrian Allen
Text Editors: David Thiemann, Russell B. Adams Jr.,
Leslie Marshall, Brooke Stoddard
Writers: Lynn R. Addison, William C. Banks, Megan
Barnett, Malachy Duffy, Steven J. Forbis, Bonnie
Bohling Kreitler, William Worsley
Copy Co-ordinator: Margery duMond
Art Assistants: George Bell, Lorraine D. Rivard,
Richard Whiting
Picture Co-ordinator: Renée DeSandies
Editorial Assistant: Susanne S. Trice

EUROPEAN EDITION
Series Director: Jackie Matthews
Writer: Charles Boyle
Designer: Paul Reeves
Sub-Editors: Sally Rowland, Hilary Hockman
Special Contributor: Susie Bicknell

EDITORIAL PRODUCTION
Chief: Ellen Brush
Production Assistants: Stephanie Lee, Jane Lillicrap
Editorial Department: Theresa John, Debra Lelliott

THE CONSULTANTS: Leslie Stokes is a self-employed carpenter and joiner
specializing in purpose-made joinery and internal fittings. Since 1976 he
has taught in the timber trades department at the Hammersmith and
West London College.

Ron Roszkiewicz, the chief consultant for this book, is an accomplished
wood craftsman who develops tool specifications and prepares catalogues
and instructional guides for a hand-tool supply company.

Contents

The Carpenter's Art

A saw in action. A circular saw, the all-purpose carpentry tool, cuts with the grain through a rough 150 by 50 mm board. The blade spins anticlockwise, spewing most of the sawdust out of the spout at the back of the saw; the blade guard has retracted under the hood of the saw, protecting the operator without interfering with the cut. Combined with home-made jigs and guides, this saw can be nearly as precise and versatile as more expensive fixed power tools such as the radial arm saw *(page 17)* or the bench saw.

Wood is the ubiquitous building material in houses. There is wood in floor joists and flooring, partitions, rafters and roof decking; and there is wood throughout the interior, in doors and doorframes, staircases, wall panelling, window frames and mouldings. Furthermore, many houses are now built with timber frames—and those that have walls of brick or stone often have a wooden skeleton.

Wood is the material of choice for good reasons: it is very strong, exceptionally durable, light in weight, weather-resistant and a good insulator. Furthermore, wood is beautiful, whether covered with paint or stained to emphasize its own striking patterns of colour, texture, grain and shadow. And from the practical viewpoint of the carpenter, wood is universally available, relatively inexpensive and capable of being shaped and assembled in an infinite variety of ways with simple tools.

The skills needed for working with wood are basic ones: sawing boards to size, making holes in them, shaping them with planes, spokeshaves, chisels and routers and joining the pieces neatly and securely with fasteners or glue. Most people have an introduction to woodworking at school, but even those who have not forgotten what the teacher taught soon discover that he did not teach enough. The craftsmanship needed to repair or renovate a house, from erecting a partition to repairing a skirting board, is unlike that needed to build a towel holder for the kitchen. House carpentry is more difficult: usually the work must be done freehand, with portable tools and home-made jigs, rather than fixed power tools that guarantee precision; and as construction timber is rougher and has a higher moisture content, it is more difficult to work than the joinery quality timber used in a workshop.

There are tricks to every basic operation—from the seemingly simple chores of driving in a nail and planing a square, straight edge, to the complications of scribing an elaborate curve and joining intricate mouldings—and mastery of these tricks distinguishes a good carpenter from an ordinary one. A generation ago, apprentice carpenters learnt the nuances of their trade by watching and imitating a master—the sort of craftsman who carried a home-made wooden toolbox, and who prided himself on his work and the daily upkeep of his tools. In this era of metal toolboxes, portable power tools and mass-produced houses, such perfectionists are a dying breed. But the keys to their craftsmanship—the small, critical techniques of handling tools the right way—remain the same. These techniques are not always easy to acquire but, once mastered, they make every job go fast and come out right.

The Carpenter's Material: Wood from Tree or Factory

"We may use wood with intelligence only if we understand it," the architect Frank Lloyd Wright once said—and he spoke for craftsmen as well as architects. The quality of a carpenter's work depends as much on his knowledge of wood as on his skill with tools.

Wood is a notoriously capricious material that can frustrate the finest workman—by tearing roughly when planed, perhaps, or by stubbornly refusing to accept a coat of paint. Such problems are so common that many people accept them with resignation. In fact, trouble can often be prevented by choosing a wood (or a wood product, such as plywood) with its particular properties in mind.

You can learn a great deal about the strength and woodworking characteristics of a board simply by looking at it. At the end of a log or a board, you can see a series of thin, concentric circles. These annual rings, one formed each year during a spurt of growth, actually consist of a pair of rings: a light-coloured one called earlywood or springwood, and a darker, denser ring called latewood or summerwood. Boards with wide rings of earlywood are generally weaker than those in which latewood is predominant.

Trees are classified as softwoods or hardwoods. Hardwood timber—which is used only for fine interior moulding, flooring and panelling, because of its high cost—comes from broad-leaved trees, which drop their leaves every autumn. Softwood timber, from needle-leaved evergreen trees, is the builder's mainstay.

Softwood is available from timber merchants or D.I.Y. outlets, either sawn or planed-all-round (PAR). Sawn timber is sold in its original rough-cut condition without having been trimmed, and is used principally for carcassing; PAR timber has been planed to make it smooth and square. Ready-machined sections of softwood for architraves, skirting boards and other moulding work are also available.

Both sawn and planed softwood are sold in standard widths and thicknesses. When buying timber for precision work, however, check the dimensions carefully: sawn timber may have shrunk slightly during its drying process, and the actual dimensions of planed boards are always about 5 mm less than the labelled, or nominal, dimensions. For example, the actual size of a planed board whose nominal dimensions are 100 by 50 mm will be 95 by 45 mm.

Hardwood is much more expensive than softwood, and is usually sold in ready-machined sections for decorative panelling and external joinery such as door and window sills. For larger requirements, hardwood is sold in slab form in non-standard sizes and priced by the cubic metre. Home-grown hardwoods are rare, and are used mainly for carving and turning.

Wood is graded into two main categories, according to its moisture content: joinery quality timber has been dried until its moisture content is no more than 15 per cent, while the figure for carcassing timber is 20 per cent. As the wood dries out, it shrinks in width and may warp slightly; joinery quality timber should therefore be used wherever the surface appearance of the wood is important.

As most timber within these two categories is sold unsorted into further grades, it is advisable when possible to select individual boards by looking for defects that may impair their strength and—where this is important—spoil their surface quality.

☐ Knots less than 20 mm wide, common in virtually all rough timber, do not weaken a board, although they may mar its appearance. Larger knots, particularly near the edge of a board, can weaken the board substantially. Such boards can be used for studs, blocking and similar jobs; they should not be used for load-bearing members such as posts, joists and rafters.

☐ Cross-grained boards, in which the grain runs at an angle to the edge rather than parallel to it, are relatively weak; use them only for non-bearing uses.

☐ Pith, the dark core of a tree trunk, weakens timber; do not use boards with visible pith for structural timber.

☐ Reaction wood—a section of a board with large gaps between annual rings and a rough, uneven grain—is found round many knots. It weakens the wood and is difficult to cut and shape with tools.

☐ Cracks in wood may be harmful or not, depending on their location. A shake—a wide crack between annual rings, caused by wind damage or decay—is a serious weakness. But checks—small cracks across the annual rings—are a purely cosmetic defect caused by uneven drying.

Factory-made wood products—chipboard, hardboard, blockboard and plywood—are free of these defects and have several other advantages over ordinary boards, particularly for covering large surfaces. These products have consistent thickness and strength, and do not warp or shrink as much as wood.

Plywood, the most common of the four, is made by gluing together several thin sheets of wood called plies, with the grain of each ply at right angles to that of the adjacent ones. Plywood is graded according to the appearance of the outer veneers on both sides of the board—the top grade is A, indicating a blemish-free surface; an average grade is B/BB, indicating that both sides have small knots and markings and one side also has plugs to replace large knots or faults. Plywood is available in a range of timbers, but birch plywood is the most common and also the strongest. Its uses range from small projects such as shelves to the construction of walls, ceilings and roofs. For work in damp conditions or outside, buy plywood stamped "EXT"; this indicates a weatherproof and boilproof standard.

Blockboard, heavier and stronger than plywood, comprises a hard core of wood strips between birch plies. In laminboard, the finest quality blockboard, the wood strips are no wider than 12 mm; the strips in ordinary blockboard may be up to 40 mm wide, and those in battenboard up to 75 mm wide. Blockboard may have either one or two plies on each side, and decorative veneers in, for example, oak, teak or sapele. It is suitable for such items as doors, table tops and wide shelves.

Hardboard is made by reducing wood to its individual fibres, then heating and compressing these fibres to form panels. It comes in two basic grades, standard and tempered. The latter is stiffer and water-resistant; it should be used for wall and ceiling linings, underlaying and finished flooring, either over boards or concrete.

Chipboard is manufactured from timber or flax particles which are compressed between heated plates to uniform density and thickness. Chipboard is cheaper than both plywood and blockboard, but it is not as strong; the standard grade is suitable for roof decking, while the flooring grade is denser and often waterproof.

Watching for Warps

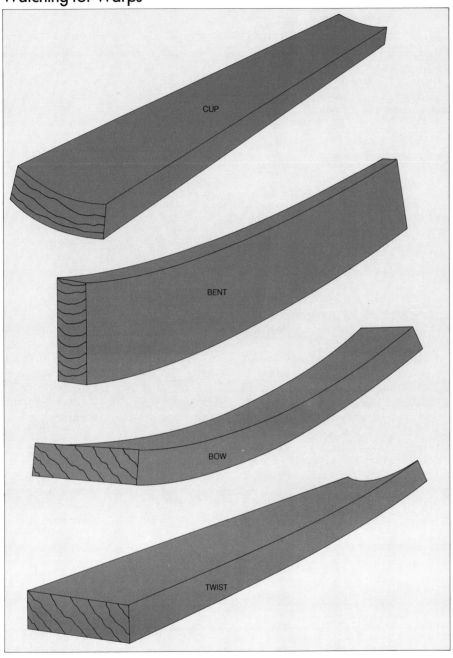

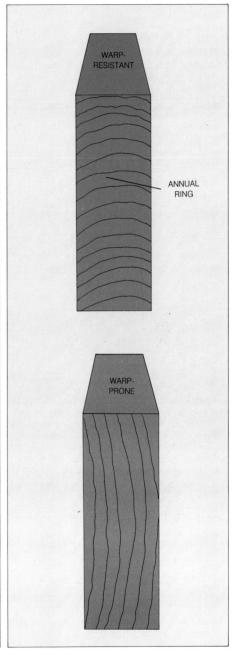

Four types of warping. Check the straightness of a board by sighting along all four of its sides. A cup—a slight curve across the width of a board—does not seriously impair its strength or usefulness for construction. A board that is bent (an end-to-end curve along an edge) or has a bow (an end-to-end curve along a face) can be used horizontally with the convex side upwards—the board will eventually straighten under the weight it bears—but should not be used vertically in a load-bearing wall. Boards with a twist are unstable and likely to distort more as they continue to dry; use them only if strength and straightness are unimportant.

Good and bad ends. Timber with the annual rings—visible as thin, concentric lines at the end of a board—parallel to its edges resists warping. Boards with the rings parallel to the faces tend to warp from seasonal changes in humidity and temperature. Do not use them where appearance or straightness is critical—in the rough framing for a door or window, for example.

The Right Way
to Store Timber

Stacking wood outdoors. Arrange timber or plywood in tight stacks, raised 100 to 150 mm above the ground on timber offcuts, then cover the stacks with a sheet of tarpaulin to keep moisture out. Lay bricks on top of the sheet and timber offcuts round its edges to anchor the cover loosely enough to let air circulate under the pile. Use the wood as soon as possible; otherwise the top boards may warp.

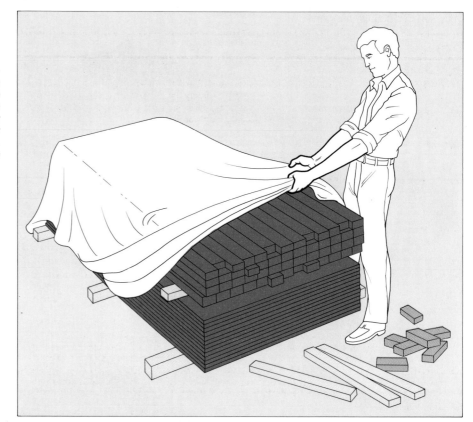

Racks for indoor storage. Build racks at 600 mm intervals; nail 100 by 50 mm uprights about 1200 mm apart to a bottom plate, nail or bolt the bottom plate to the floor and nail the uprights to the exposed floor joists overhead or to a top plate fastened to the ceiling. Drill matching 30 mm holes through each upright at 250 mm intervals and slide 25 mm steel pipes through the holes to support the timber. Two racks will support boards up to 1200 mm long; for timber up to 2500 mm long use three racks and for longer boards use four racks.

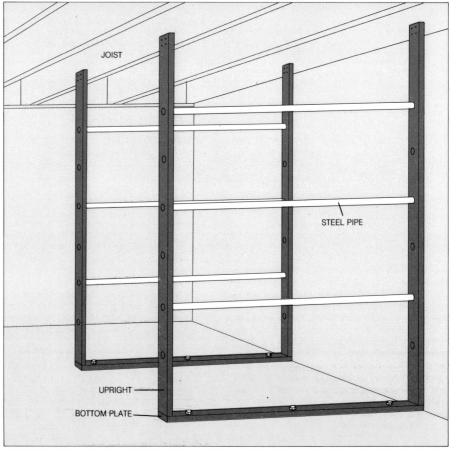

JOIST

STEEL PIPE

UPRIGHT

BOTTOM PLATE

The Qualities of Woods

Material	Characteristics
SOFTWOODS	
Douglas fir	Also known as British Columbia Pine. The preferred softwood for load-bearing members because of its exceptional strength and relatively low cost, Douglas fir is fairly heavy and holds fasteners well. It should not be used for visible woodwork: it tends to split when exposed to the elements, does not take paint well and tears badly when shaped with tools. Used extensively in the manufacture of external grade plywood.
Hemlock	One of the stiffest and strongest of the softwoods. Used for rafters and floor joists, and also for flooring and doors. Hemlock tends to split and does not take paint or hold nails well.
Larch	A standard construction timber, prized for its strength and nail-holding characteristics. It is heavy, fairly hard and quite rigid. This wood should not be used for exposed moulding; it has many small knots, shrinks badly, splinters and tears when shaped with tools, and often splits when nailed. Closely resembles Douglas fir.
Parana pine	Commonly used in stairways and rough framing because of its great strength. Parana pine is heavy, harder than any other softwood, and very rigid; it shrinks a great deal as it dries but is stable afterwards. This wood holds fasteners well, but is difficult to shape with tools, tends to split when exposed to the weather and does not hold paint well.
Redwood	Term often used to describe similar woods such as Scots pine, red pine and red deal, usually imported from the Baltic countries. Commonly used for roofing members, cladding, machined sections, indoor mouldings, and so-called "pine" furniture, because of its combination of beauty, strength and resistance to decay. Redwood is light, stable, fairly rigid and fairly hard; it is easy to shape, glue and paint.
Western red cedar	Used for exterior cladding and fence posts, because of its unusual resistance to rot. It is light, soft and very weak. Cedar is easy to shape with tools, is usually stable and bonds well with glue and paint; it does not hold nails well.
Whitewood	Like redwood, whitewood covers a number of similar species, such as fir, spruce and white pine. Primarily used for rough framing and flooring. It is soft and light, very easy to cut and holds fasteners well.
HARDWOODS	
Iroko	Used for fine joinery, worktops, parquet flooring and garden furniture. This rather coarse wood is fairly easily available and relatively inexpensive.
Japanese oak	Used for flooring, doors, panelling and interior moulding. Oak is heavy, hard and very strong; it is difficult to shape with tools and does not bond well with glue. This wood holds nails well, although it tends to split when nailed; pilot holes must be used.
Mahogany	This strong wood has good finishing qualities and is used for fine interior joinery and panelling. There are many sources, including Africa, South America and the Philippines. Sometimes known under different names such as Sapele and Utile.
Ramin	Used for mouldings and interior joinery. One of the most common, least expensive and softest hardwoods available. Ramin, unlike most other hardwoods which need pilot holes or should be glued, can be nailed easily. Tends to stain and does not bend well.
Teak	Used for furniture, fine joinery, sheds, gates and turning. Teak is good for bending and very resistant to fungi and insects. Slow machine speeds must be used to prevent tools blunting and overheating.
MANUFACTURED BOARDS	
Blockboard	Used for interior work only, such as worktops, doors, fitted units and shelving. The quality of the surface veneer depends on the width of the core strips. Laminboard—cores up to 12 mm—gives the best finish, whereas battenboard—cores up to 75 mm—has a tendency to ripple. Holds fasteners and glue well, except on the core end-grain.
Chipboard	Used for underlayment shelving and flooring. Chipboard is generally heavier and slightly stronger than hardboard. Panels can be cut and glued easily but tend to split when nailed on the edges and are difficult to paint. To fasten, use twinfast chipboard screws.
Hardboard	Used for cladding, interior panelling, wall and ceiling linings and floor underlayment. Hardboard is fairly heavy, hard and somewhat brittle. It is easy to shape with tools, though it shreds when cut; it takes glue and paint well but does not hold fasteners.
Plywood	Used for subflooring, wall and roof decking, exterior cladding, interior panelling and shelving. Heavy, fairly hard and much stronger than chipboard and hardboard, plywood is easy to cut and shape, and takes glue well; fasteners hold well when driven into the face.

Special properties for special needs. The first column of this chart lists the woods commonly used in house construction, grouped in three categories, and the second describes the applications and characteristics. Woods that do not respond to changes of humidity are called stable; if a wood tends to swell, warp or split when the humidity changes, the particular fault is indicated. To use the chart, match the characteristics of the woods available in your area to the requirements of your job. Decay-resistant woods such as redwood and cedar are good choices for outdoor work; Douglas fir and Parana pine are best for important structural parts of a house because of their strength.

A Clean and Simple Cut across the Grain

A cut straight across the grain of wood is the most common cut in carpentry, for a simple reason: the grain runs with the length of a board and standard-length boards generally must be shortened. Fortunately, such crosscutting, at 90 degrees to the board edge, is also the easiest cut: it is generally a short one, and the teeth of a crosscut-saw blade need only slice the wood fibres, a cut that requires less effort than the chopping and ripping performed by a rip saw *(pages 20–25)*.

Which tool to use for crosscutting depends on the precision required and the volume and location of the job.

Most of these cuts—particularly in carcassing timber—can be made with a portable electric circular saw. For precise work on finishes, you need a stiff-bladed tenon saw and a mitre box. Both rough and precise cuts across the grain can be made quickly and easily with a radial arm power saw *(pages 17–19)*. The crosscut handsaw is still sometimes necessary—for rough cuts in cramped areas, for jobs where there is no electricity, and for boards that are too short to be steadied safely for a power saw.

When you buy new tools, there are certain features to look for. The teeth of a crosscut handsaw are set alternately to the left and right of the plane of the blade and are not only pointed, but also bevelled front to back *(page 44)*. A better blade is wider near the teeth, to keep the kerf from binding the blade. A blade with 10 teeth—"points"—per 25 mm is generally useful; an 8-point saw makes quicker but rougher cuts.

While every carpenter owns a handsaw, he most often uses a portable circular saw, which makes rough cuts nearly instantly and, with a simple jig, cuts lengths very accurately. A model with a 1,000 watt motor and a blade of 180 mm diameter, which can saw completely through a 100 by 50 mm board at a 45 degree angle, is adequate for home use. Circular saws are very dangerous tools, and must be used with careful attention to safety.

Most circular saws come equipped with a combination blade which serves for general-purpose cutting *(page 45)*; its teeth are a compromise between the designs used for crosscut and rip handsaws, and the blade is excellent for fast crosscutting. If you do a great deal of cutting, however, you may want to substitute a more expensive blade that has carbide tips brazed to its teeth—the carbide-tipped blade makes a slightly wider kerf than an ordinary steel one, but it stays sharp more than 10 times as long. For smoother cuts use a crosscut blade *(page 44)*, whose fine pointed teeth are just like those of the crosscut handsaw. This blade slices the wood more slowly than the combination blade, but leaves a much better finish. Set the cutting depth for any of these blades so that one entire tooth will protrude below the bottom of the board you cut.

Even in a jig, a circular saw cannot match the accuracy of a mitre box guiding a tenon saw, its fine-toothed blade reinforced to keep the cut straight. For good work you need more than the simple, slotted boxes of wood or plastic that sell for a few pounds. Versatile models such as the one shown on the cover—made of metal and able to accommodate boards 80 to 100 mm thick and 100 to 200 mm wide at any angle—are available at prices that range from modest to high. In them, the saw slides within guides and can be locked in a raised position while you align a board on the frame below. Any mitre box should be anchored to a workbench; use bolts and wing nuts so that it can be easily removed for work elsewhere.

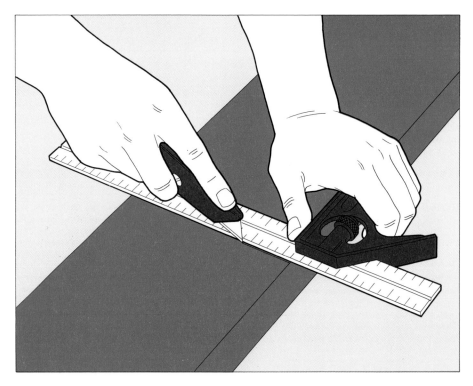

Marking a crosscut. For most 90 degree crosscuts, hold the handle of a combination square firmly against the edge of the board and mark along the blade. For rough work, use a pencil; for finer work, score the wood several times with the point of a trimming knife—the scored line is sharper and will help to prevent splintering as the wood is cut.

Crosscutting with a Handsaw

1 **Beginning the cut.** Lay a board across two saw-horses, steady it with the knee opposite your cutting arm and grip the handle of the saw so that your index finger rests along the blade to help keep the saw course true. Set the heel, or handle end, of the blade on the board edge at an angle of about 20 degrees. For rough work, the teeth should lie directly on a pencilled line; for fine work, on the waste side of a knife mark.

Holding the thumb of your free hand against the blade as a guide, draw the saw half way back towards you, pressing lightly to cut into the wood. Lift the blade from the wood, reset it to the starting position, and then pull backwards again; do this several times until the kerf is at least as deep as the teeth. Then lengthen and deepen the kerf with short, smooth back-and-forth strokes that cut in both directions.

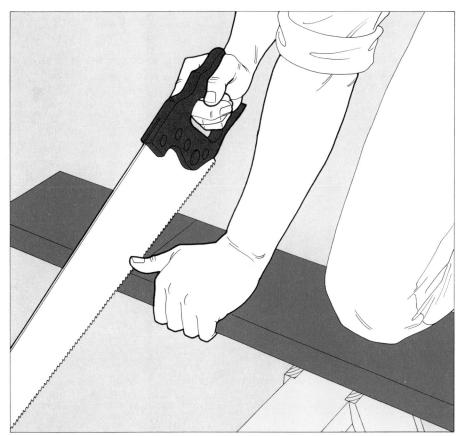

2 **Cutting through the board.** When the kerf is about 25 mm long—sufficient to establish the direction of the cut—gradually increase the angle of the saw to 45 degrees and lengthen your strokes, cutting mainly on the forward stroke and using moderate pressure. Use most of the full length of the saw, from about 80 mm from the tip nearly to the handle. Try to let the saw feel as if it is cutting on its own, and do not force the blade. When the cut is almost complete, reach over the top of the saw to support the waste piece so that it does not fall and splinter the wood.

If the saw binds in green or warped wood, rub beeswax or candlewax on the blade or drive a wedge into the kerf behind the blade. If the blade twists and binds as you try to correct a straying cut, begin the cut at a new spot or widen the old kerf by resawing it until you reach uncut wood.

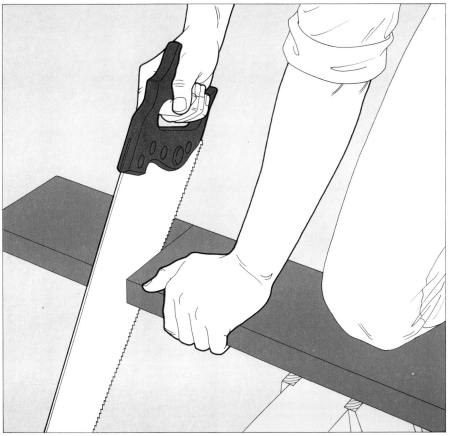

Freehand Cuts with a Circular Saw

1 Aligning the saw. Lay the board across two sawhorses and steady it with a foot or knee, depending on the height of the sawhorses and your sense of balance. Or you can clamp the board to one sawhorse. Place the front of the base plate on the board with the blade at least 10 mm from the board edge, and hold the saw so that the entire plate is level; then use the guide in the base plate, or the blade itself, to align the blade with the cutting line.

The guide in the base plate is generally an effective device for aligning a straight cut, but after you change or sharpen the blade, the guide itself may not line up properly with the teeth of the blade. Experience with your own saw will tell you how to compensate for a misaligned base-plate guide or whether to use it at all.

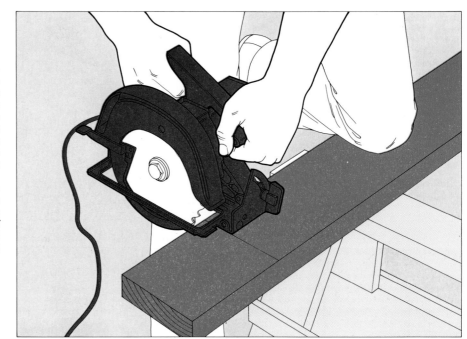

2 Making the cut. Start the saw and, applying pressure forwards but not downwards, push the blade smoothly into the board, watching the guide or blade to be sure that the blade cuts along the line. Near the end of the cut, slow the forward motion, then quickly push through the remainder of the board in a single stroke. Immediately release the switch and move the saw away from the board, checking to be certain that the blade guard returns to its closed position.

If the blade binds or goes off course, release the switch immediately and wait for the blade to stop moving. Pull the blade from the kerf, reset it to the starting position and start sawing again, cutting slowly into the kerf. Allow the blade to work its own way—with minimal pressure forwards—through the wood that was binding it before, or through new wood along the cutting line to correct a wayward first cut.

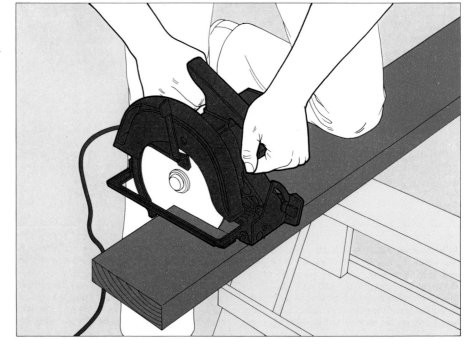

A Guide and a Jig
for Accurate Speed

A square for right angles. Hold the long leg of a carpenter's square against the far edge of the board and set the base plate against the outer edge of the short leg. Slide saw and square along the board until the blade aligns with the cutting line, then make the cut by moving the saw along the short leg of the square.

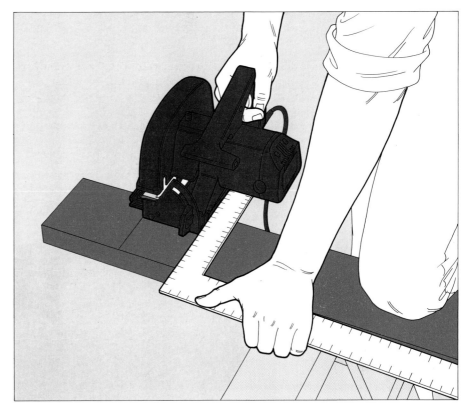

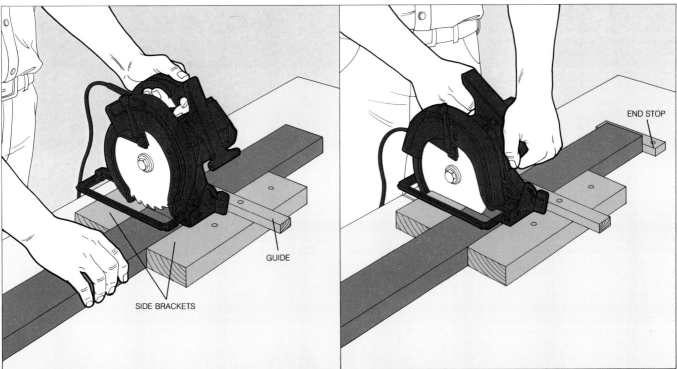

A jig for cuts of equal length. Set the marked board that you are going to cut on a sheet of plywood and bracket it with two long wood offcuts as thick as the piece to be cut; nail these side brackets to the plywood. Nail a wood-strip guide across the top of the offcuts at right angles to the board and set the saw, with its blade fully elevated, against the guide *(above, left)*. Slide the board beneath the saw until the cutting line is below the blade, then, at the far end of the board, nail a block of wood to the plywood as an end stop. Set the blade to the proper depth and cut through the board and the side brackets by running the saw along the guide *(above, right)*. To cut more boards to the same length, slip one at a time into the jig and against the stop.

To cut several pieces at once—for example, to cut boards into fence pickets—widen the jig to hold the pieces side by side and make a long stop exactly parallel to the guide.

A Mitre Box for Precision

1 Setting the angle. With the blade raised, release the catch of the mitre box's angle-setting knob and move the point to the 90 degree mark. Position the cutting line of the board approximately beneath the blade, release the front and back sawguide catches and then, holding the blade 5 mm above the board, make a final adjustment in the position of the cutting line.

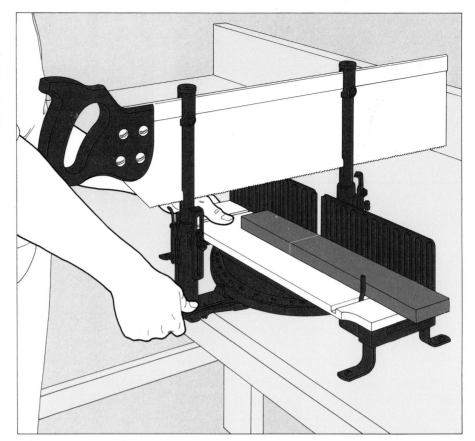

2 Making the cut. With a thumb and a mitre-box cramp, steady the board against the frame. Begin the kerf with several backward strokes, as for any crosscut, but hold the saw level to cut the entire upper surface of the wood along the cutting line. Then, cutting on both forward and backward strokes, cut the rest of the way through the board. Use long, smooth strokes that fall just short of pulling the blade from the rear guide or running the handle into the front guide.

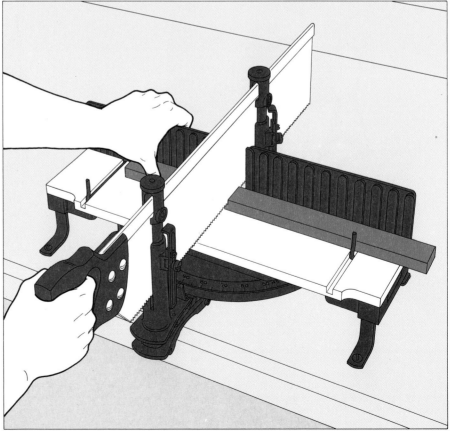

The Versatile Radial Arm Saw

The multijointed fixed power tool called a radial arm saw is one of the most versatile, useful and ingeniously designed of all machines for working with wood. While it is expensive—five to 10 times the price of a portable circular saw—it can make any cut that could be made with a handsaw, circular saw or mitre box, but with a combination of speed and precision that is not found in any one of the other tools. It is the preferred shop tool for carpentry; it is better adapted than a bench saw for cutting many boards to the same length and angle, as in rough framing, or for making many cuts through large pieces of moulding.

The blade and motor of the saw ride above a worktable along the track of a horizontal arm. Cutting is always above the table, where the blade position is clearly visible, and crosscutting is simple—you pull the saw by its handle straight towards you until the board is cut, then push the saw back. But the arm that supports the saw can also pivot more than 180 degrees over the table and the saw can tilt on this arm to any angle: the pivoting and tilting together can position the blade for a cut at any angle. Scales and locks are used to adjust the blade settings with the accuracy of a mitre box; safety guards on either side shield the blade itself.

Crosscutting blades for a radial arm saw include the standard combination steel blade and the long-lasting carbide-tipped blade, both described on page 12. For fine cutting, especially for moulding, use a planer blade, which is slower but makes an extremely smooth cut.

Most radial arm saws come equipped with a warp-resistant chipboard table top. Protect this table surface—which otherwise will be gouged as the blade penetrates the first board being cut—with a layer of 6 mm plywood stuck down with contact adhesive. Cover the edges of the plywood layer with masking tape, so as to prevent splinters from snagging your clothes. Place tables at the sides of the saw to support long boards.

Since both the plywood cover on the table surface and the replaceable wooden "fence" that helps to hold boards in place are going to be cut by the blade in use, many craftsmen prepare the plywood cover and the wooden fence for use by making crosscuts, angle cuts *(page 26)* and rip cuts

(page 22) in them in advance. Such preparatory cuts will then help the user to align boards for accurate cutting and speed up the work in hand.

In addition to the plywood cover, there are other accessories that increase the saw's usefulness. A wooden block placed as a stop at a fixed distance from the blade helps when you need to cut many pieces to the same length. An extra tall guide, or fence, used as a temporary replacement for the standard fence, will help you when you need to cut accurately through several boards simultaneously.

Safety Tips for Radial Arm Saw Crosscuts

☐ Do all your planning before starting the motor; concentrate completely on the cut being made, and turn the motor off as soon as the cut is finished.

☐ Hold the board being cut firmly against the fence, keeping your hand well away from the blade. Never allow fingers to rest on the back of the fence.

☐ Pull the blade forward only until its bottom edge emerges from the wood; push the saw immediately to its rear position and then turn it off.

(For safety in rip-cutting, see page 23.)

Anatomy of a Radial Arm Saw

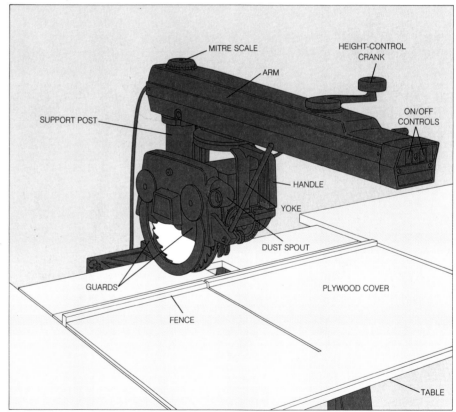

A versatile cutter. This saw, whose downward-cutting teeth face away from you for a crosscut and towards you for a rip cut, is suspended with its motor in a yoke that permits it to tilt 100 degrees right or left. The yoke can also turn more than 360 degrees in its swivel mount, which rides in a track beneath a horizontal arm. The arm can move as well—manually 105 degrees to both right and left, or up and down when you turn a height-control crank that adjusts the arm's support post. A mitre scale shows the angle of the blade in relation to a replaceable wooden fence against which the board to be cut is set. A replaceable plywood sheet covers the worktable.

In use the saw is pulled from back to front along its track in the arm, the blade cutting through first the fence and then the board as it skims the plywood table cover. Upper and lower guards shield the blade, and a dust spout directs sawdust to the side. Other scales, locks and safety features are provided for angle cuts *(pages 26–29)* and rip cuts *(pages 20–25)*.

The Basic Set-up
for a Crosscut

1 **Setting up the job.** With the motor off and in the rear position, set the arm at 0 degrees on the mitre scale and the blade 3 mm below the level of the plywood table covering. Place the board against the fence, positioned so that the blade will cut on the waste side of the cutting line. Rest the fingers of your left hand on the board at least 150 mm from the cutting line, and press the board against the fence with your thumb.

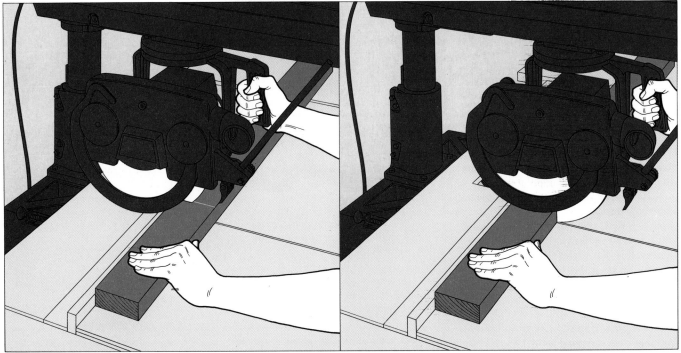

2 **Making the cut.** Start the motor and, keeping a firm grip on the handle, pull the saw into the board *(above, left)*; if the blade tends to climb over the board and bind there, lock your elbow by straightening your arm. When the bottom of the blade emerges from the front edge of the board *(above, right)*, return the saw to the rear position and shut off the power. If you pull the blade completely through the cut board, the saw teeth

moving upwards at the rear may catch the waste piece and hurl it over the fence.

If you cannot keep the blade from climbing over the board, shut off the power immediately and then start the cut again, this time in two passes. For the first pass, raise the blade to make a kerf about half as deep as the board; for the second pass, position the saw at the normal cutting height.

Special Arrangements for Awkward Jobs

Stops for repeated cuts. To crosscut a number of long boards one after the other to the same length, nail a 100 by 50 mm block that is chamfered—bevelled—at the bottom to keep sawdust from building up and distorting your measurement, to a worktable at the side of the saw *(below, left)*. The block acts as a stop, as in cuts made with a circular saw *(page 15, bottom)*.

As a stop for short boards, fasten a woodworker's cramp to the saw fence, leaving a gap below the cramp for accumulations of sawdust *(below, right)*.

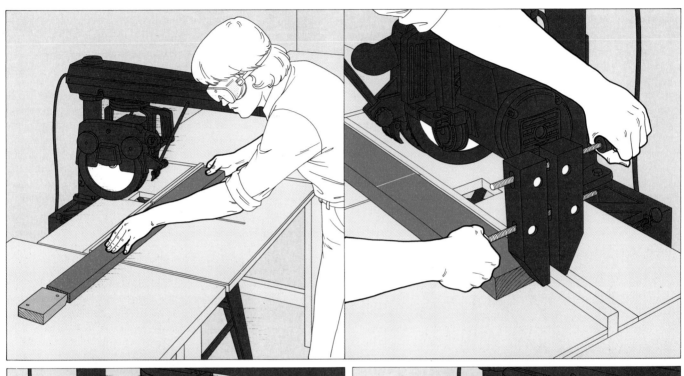

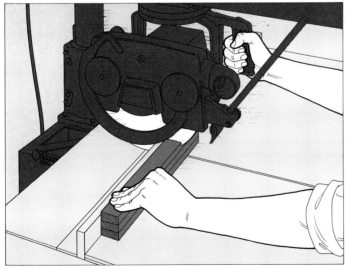

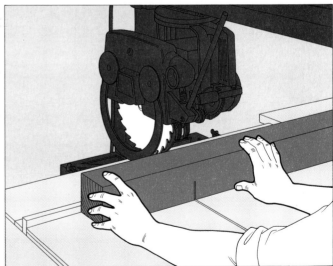

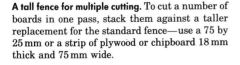

A tall fence for multiple cutting. To cut a number of boards in one pass, stack them against a taller replacement for the standard fence—use a 75 by 25 mm or a strip of plywood or chipboard 18 mm thick and 75 mm wide.

Cutting thick timber. To crosscut a board that is as much as twice as thick as the distance between motor and blade teeth, raise the blade until the motor clears the board to be cut, then make a first cut. Turn the board over, align the kerf you have made in it with the blade *(above)*, and pull the saw through for the final cut.

Sawing with the Grain for a Rip Cut

Cutting a board lengthwise, with the grain, in what is known as rip cutting, used to be a major part of a carpenter's work. It is no longer so—modern sawmills cut and plane boards to the standard dimensions of house carpentry—but many boards must still be trimmed to width on the job. Among them are stair treads and risers, odd-sized jambs for plaster walls, and new studs cut to match old, full-sized timber.

None of these jobs is easy. A rip cut, which chops and tears the fibres of a board, requires about five times as much work as a crosscut, which neatly severs the fibres. It is harder to keep straight, because the saw blade tends to follow the grain, which is never quite true. And it leaves a rough edge that must be planed smooth on exposed pieces of wood; in marking such pieces for a cut, an extra 2 mm should be allowed for the planing.

Most rip cuts are now made with power saws, but a handsaw remains the only suitable tool when a board is already nailed in place in a hard-to-reach spot, or when a piece of wood is too small to be cut safely with a power saw. The preferred hand tool is a 5 or 6-point ripsaw, which has teeth designed specifically for efficient rip cuts *(opposite page, top)*; an alternative is an 8-point crosscut saw, which is slower but more commonly available.

A portable circular saw, the standard ripping tool, is fast and durable but not particularly precise, even in skilled hands, when the cut is made freehand. For somewhat more accurate results, you can use the rip guide shown overleaf; on boards more than 300 mm wide, use one of the panel-cutting guides shown on page 33. For all of these cutting methods, the power saw is fitted with the same blade that is used for cross-cutting—a steel combination blade (or its carbide-tipped equivalent). Alternatively, use a special rip-cut blade *(page 45)*, which has slightly more hooked teeth than those of a combination blade, enabling it to chisel through the wood more quickly. Pitch and resins gradually build up on either type of blade until it sticks in the kerf; these deposits are easy to remove with paraffin or commercial solvents.

The radial arm saw is the best tool to use for both speed of production and precision; it can rip with either of these blades, but a rip-cut blade will give easier, cleaner cuts. The saw is easily set up for ripping *(pages 22–25)*, but to cut long pieces, you will need to slide boards along worktables that you have placed on each side of the saw table.

Three Ways to Mark for a Rip

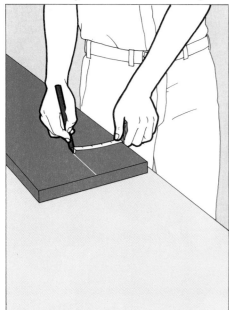

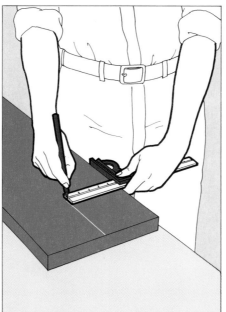

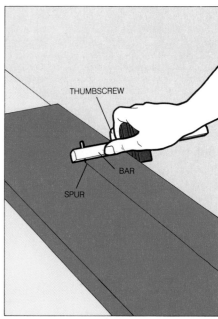

A steel tape for rough work. Hold the tape case in the palm of one hand, extend the tape to the measurement for the cut, and set the case next to the edge of the board, with your forefinger tight against the edge; with the fingers of your other hand, hold a pencil against the end of the tape—many tapes have a V-shaped notch there. Slide both hands smoothly along the board; use your forefinger as a guide, keep the tape perpendicular to the edge and keep the length constant by clamping your fingers firmly on the tape.

A combination square for convenience. Extend the blade of the square to the measurement for the cut and lock it with the knurled nut in the handle. Set the square, machined face of the handle tight against the edge of the board with one hand and hold a pencil against the end of the blade with the other; many blades have a groove here that will help hold the pencil. Slide the square and pencil along the board together to mark the cut, holding the machined face of the square tight against the edge of the board.

A marking gauge for precision. Mark the start of the cut at one end of the board. Hold the head of the marking gauge flat against the edge of the board, slide the bar out until its spur touches the mark and tighten the thumbscrew on the head. Hold the head of the gauge in your palm and roll it forward until the spur barely touches the board, then push the gauge along the board; press the head firmly sideways against the edge and brace the bar with your thumb. The spur should score a clear, shallow line.

The Old-Fashioned Way: Ripping with a Handsaw

Using a ripsaw. Set a small board on a sawhorse as you would for a crosscut; support a large one between two sawhorses. Start the cut as you would a crosscut *(page 13, Step 1)*; then, when the cut is about 25 mm long, raise the angle of the saw to about 60 degrees and apply most of the force on the push stroke. If the blade buckles or skips through the cut, lower the angle of the saw slightly; if the board pinches the blade, tap wooden wedges into the kerf *(inset)*.

When using one sawhorse, edge the board forward little by little; half way through the cut, turn the board around and saw from the other end. When using two sawhorses, cut to within a few centimetres of a horse, then slide the board back and cut on the other side of the horse.

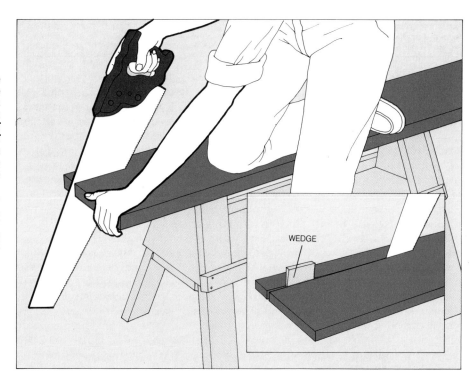

WEDGE

Ripping with a Circular Saw

A freehand cut. Clamp or tack the board to two sawhorses and set the saw blade 6 mm deeper than the thickness of the board. Rest the saw nose flat on the end of the board and align the base-plate guide mark or the blade itself with the cutting line, then start the saw and slowly push it into the board. Near the end of the cut, a base-plate guide mark will slide off the end of the board; guide the saw by the blade alone.

If the saw motor slows and labours, pause until it gains speed, then push it forward more slowly. If the cut goes off the line, angle the saw slightly towards the line for approximately 100 mm, then straighten it when the cut returns to the line. If the blade binds, turn off the saw and tap in a wedge near the blade *(above, inset)*.

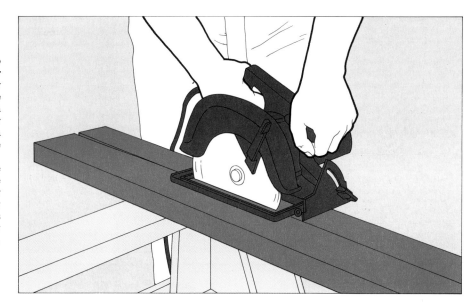

Safety Tips for Circular-Saw Rips

☐ Stand to one side of the saw, not directly behind it. If the saw kicks back—a common occurrence in a rip cut—your leg could be gashed.
☐ Do not rest your fingers on the kerf; it is the path of a possible kickback.

☐ Do not hold the waste piece with your hand; let the sawhorses support it or let it fall as it comes away.
☐ Wear goggles to protect your eyes from the large amounts of sawdust filling the air around a rip cut.

Using a rip guide. With the saw unplugged, set the nose of the base plate flat on the board and align the blade with the marked line. Slide the arm of the guide through its base-plate holder until the guide shoe fits against the edge of the board, then tighten the guide arm in position. When you make the cut, maintain a gentle sideways pressure on the saw to keep the guide shoe tight against the edge of the board.

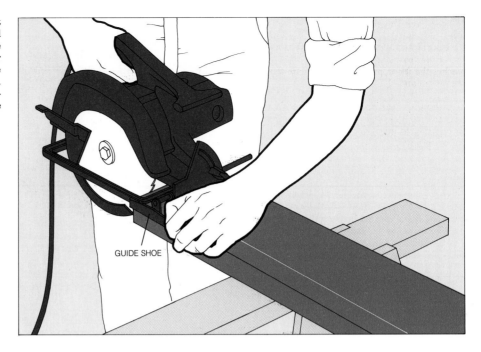

GUIDE SHOE

Ripping with a Radial Arm Saw

1 Setting the "in-rip" position. With the motor off and the blade depth set 3 mm below the top of the table covering, pull the saw forwards to the end of the arm and tighten the rip lock. Start the motor, grip the saw handle with your left hand and release the yoke lock with your right. Pivot the motor slowly to the right with both hands cutting a shallow quarter circle into the plywood table covering; at the end of the quarter circle, a cog in the yoke mechanism will lock the blade parallel to the fence, in the in-rip position—that is, with the motor away from the fence. Leave the motor on and proceed immediately to Step 2.

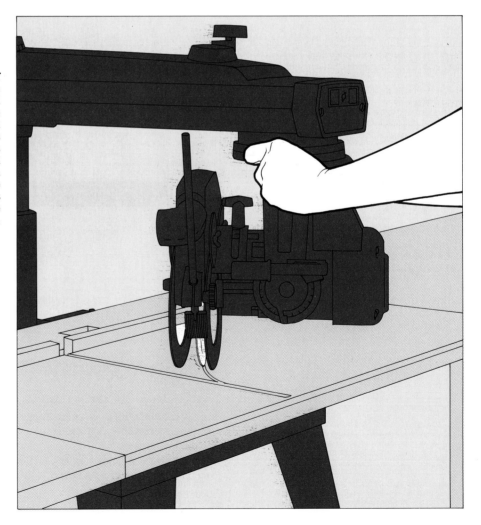

2 **Making the rip troughs.** Release the rip lock and, using both hands, slowly push the saw towards the back of the table, cutting a shallow trough in the table covering. When the blade guard reaches the fence, pull the yoke back to the end of the arm and tighten the rip lock.

Release the yoke lock and pivot the yoke 180 degrees to the "out-rip" position *(inset)*—that is, put the motor next to the fence. Loosen the rip lock and slowly push the saw back, making a second trough that runs into the end of the first.

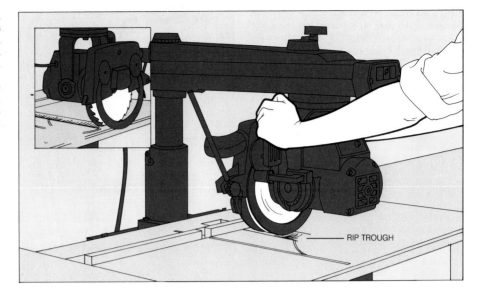

RIP TROUGH

Setting the Saw and Making the Cut

1 **Setting the width of the cut.** Turn the saw motor off. To cut a width less than 200 mm, move the yoke to the in-rip position and lock the yoke cramp *(page 17, bottom)*; for wider cuts, move the yoke to the out-rip position. Push the yoke along the arm until the pointer on the arm's rip scale shows the correct width, and tighten the rip cramp. For absolute precision, lift the guard closest to the fence and measure the cut width between the fence and the edge of a blade tooth set towards the fence *(inset)*.

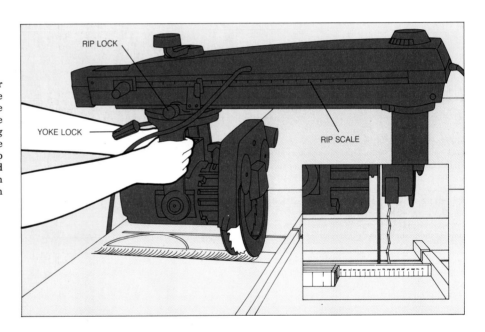

RIP LOCK

YOKE LOCK

RIP SCALE

Safety Tips for Radial Arm Saw Rips

In addition to the basic safety rules on page 17, observe these precautions:
☐ Wear goggles.
☐ Set and test the guard and antikick-back fingers *(overleaf, Steps 2 and 3)* before you make a cut.
☐ Feed the saw from the right when in-ripping, the left when out-ripping.
☐ Stand beside, not behind, the board.
☐ Do not let a helper push the board against the fence on the far side of the blade; the pressure can pinch the kerf round the blade and cause a kickback.
☐ Keep your fingers at least 50 mm from the blade; never insert them underneath the guard.
☐ Do not reach near the blade to move the waste piece when the cut is completed; push it with a scrap of timber or pull it from the other side of the blade.

2 **Adjusting the guard.** Place the board in front of the blade and loosen the wing nut that locks the guard to the motor. Rotate the guard until the spring clip on its nose is 3 mm above the board, then tighten the wing nut, locking the guard.

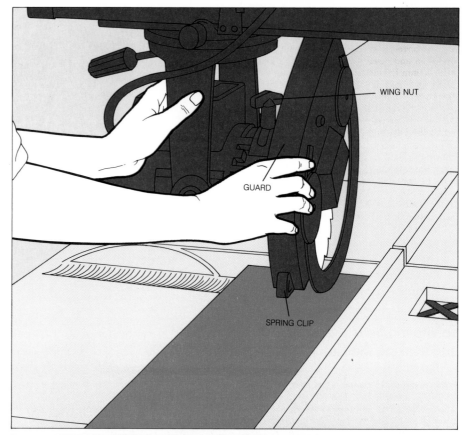

WING NUT

GUARD

SPRING CLIP

3 **Setting the antikickback fingers.** Place the board (or a scrap of the same thickness) alongside the antikickback fingers at the back of the guard. The fingers hang from the end of a rod; loosen the cramp that fastens this rod to the guard, lower the rod until the fingers dangle 3 mm below the top of the board and tighten the cramp. To test the fingers, lift them and place the board underneath, then push the board towards the blade (*inset*); the fingers should bite into the top of the board and prevent it from moving backwards. If the fingers do not grab the board, adjust the rod until they do.

Some radial arm saws have the antikickback fingers positioned to the front rather than the back of the blade guard. These models have a riving knife—to prevent the blade binding—which must be lowered into position before rip cutting. Follow the manufacturer's instructions carefully, as it is most important to position the fingers and knife correctly for complete safety.

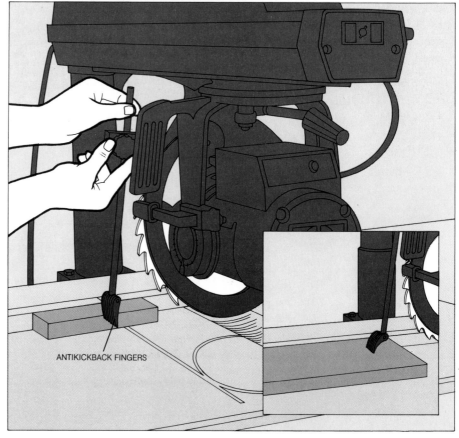

ANTIKICKBACK FINGERS

4 **Starting the cut.** Set the board flat against the fence, on the right side of the table for in-ripping, the left for out-ripping (the drawing on the right shows the correct position for an in-rip cut). Turn the saw on and place your hands on the board about 450 mm behind the blade, with one hand next to the fence and the other on the near edge of the board. Slowly push the board into the blade with the hand next to the fence; use your other hand to press the board gently down and towards the fence but do not push.

When your hands are about 150 mm from the blade, move them back along the board and resume the cut. When your hands are on the end of the board and 150 mm from the blade, proceed directly to Step 5.

If the blade binds, shut off the saw and drive a wedge into the kerf about 50 mm behind the antikickback fingers.

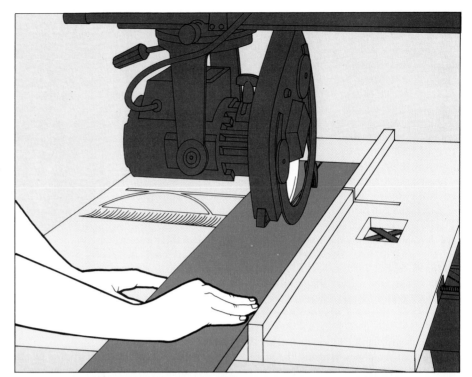

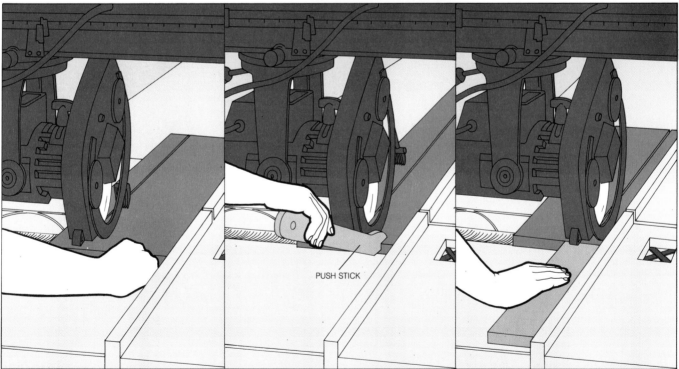

PUSH STICK

5 **Completing the cut.** If more than 150 mm of the board lies between the blade and the fence, you can complete the cut by hand *(above, left)*. Place the hand nearest the fence at the end of the board, with the thumb tucked under the palm, and take your other hand away from the board. Push the board through the saw, keeping your fingers together and your hand tight against the fence, well away from the blade and guard; then move your hand behind the fence, pull it back and turn off the motor.

If 25 to 150 mm of the board lies between the blade and the fence, use a push stick *(above, centre)*. Cut a notch at one end of a scrap of 25 mm timber 400 mm long. Set the notch on the end of the board, centred between the blade and the fence, and push the board through the saw; then move the stick and your hand behind the fence and pull them back. If the distance between the board and the fence is less than 25 mm *(above, right)*, place an offcut of wood about 400 mm long and 75 mm wide at the end of the board and against the fence. Feed the offcut part of the way through the saw, cutting the offcut while at the same time pushing the board past the saw blade, then, finally, slide the offcut back along the fence.

The Angle Cuts: Mitre, Bevel and Compound

All the myriad angled cuts required in carpentry fall into three basic types. A mitre cut, like the one on a rafter end at a roof peak, slants across the face of a board. A bevel cut slants across an edge of a board between opposite faces, as in the top of a gable stud cut to fit the pitch of a roof. And a compound cut, used primarily for joints in finishes and mouldings, combines the first two types to provide a board mitred across its face and bevelled across its edge.

Angle cuts are made with the same tools used for square cuts—the crosscut handsaw, the circular saw, the radial arm saw, and the mitre box with saw—but the techniques differ somewhat. When using a handsaw to cut an angle, for example, you may want to clamp a guide to the work to prevent the saw from slipping sideways along the board. To start a rough angle cut with a circular saw, you must lift the blade guard; and since the base plate tilts only as

far as 45 degrees in one direction, you must calculate and cut a complementary angle to make a sharper bevel than 45 degrees *(opposite page, bottom)*. With the mitre box and saw—used for the delicate work of cutting finishes such as architraves and skirting boards—you must position the wood on edge to make a bevel cut.

For any angle cut with any type of tool, you must take special pains to lay out the work for precision of fit. Generally you can hold one board against another and trace the line of their intersection. In other cases no measurement is needed because the angle is calculated in degrees or is obvious—a 45 degree mitre on a door or window architrave, for example. Often, however, you must measure with a protractor and a sliding bevel—a wooden handle bolted to a pivoted metal blade.

For simple angle cuts, fit a sliding bevel into an angle you wish to copy, lock the

blade and hold the tool against a board to mark the cut. To set a circular saw for a bevel cut, hold a sliding bevel against the saw blade—with the saw unplugged—while you adjust the tilt. In situations where it is difficult to align the saw blade by eye but you have a scale on the tool—as in setting a radial arm saw for a bevel cut—use the sliding bevel to transfer the angle to a scrap of wood, use a protractor to measure it and set the scale of the tool to the measured angle.

The scales on tools are supposed to align exactly with the saw blade, so that a simple setting cuts the angle you want. They rarely do. While the error generally is small—around 1 degree—it is enough to spoil a visible joint, and it changes as the tool is used. Test periodically to determine the correction needed. For any angle cut requiring special precision, make a test cut on a scrap and check the result with a protractor.

Making Mitres in Rough Timber

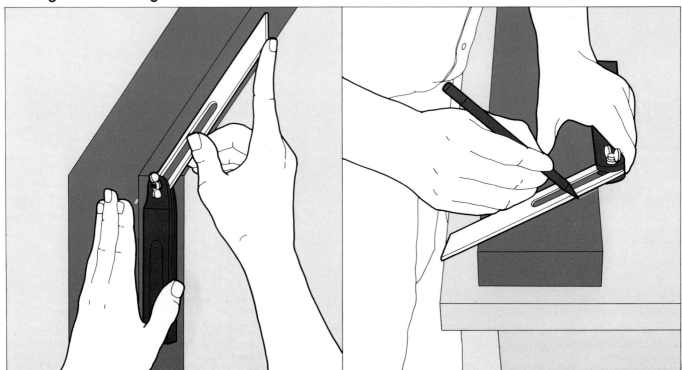

Transferring an angle. Extend the blade of a sliding bevel and adjust the wing nut on the handle so that the blade moves easily but does not swing free. Fit the sliding bevel into the angle you plan to transfer *(above, left)* with the blade corresponding to the line you are going to cut, and tighten the wing nut. Hold the handle of the sliding bevel against the edge and the blade across the face of the board to be cut, then mark the cutting line along the blade *(above, right)*.

Cutting an angle with a handsaw. If you are unsure of your ability to follow the cutting line of an angle cut, which is more difficult to start accurately than a straight cut, clamp a piece of scrap—100 by 50 mm will do—to the stock so that it is exactly lined up with the cutting line and overlaps each edge. Begin the cut as you would a square crosscut *(page 13)*. After you have established the kerf, remove the saw from the stock and check to be sure you are following the cutting line. If you are not, restart the kerf.

Cutting an angle with a circular saw. A guide tacked parallel to the cutting mark on the non-waste side of the mark is generally advisable for long cuts and is also helpful on short ones. Rest the base plate of the saw against the guide; then, before turning on the power, lift the blade guard. Hold the guard up as you begin the cut, and release it after it has cleared the edge of the board. Use the guide to keep the blade aligned, but if it strays, start the cut again: do not attempt to force it back on course.

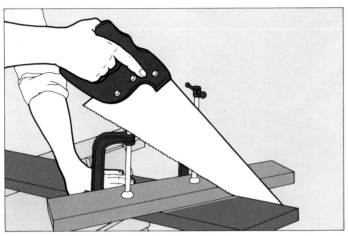

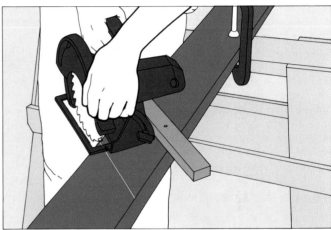

Using a Circular Saw for Bevel and Compound Angles

Setting the blade for a bevel cut. While a handsaw makes this cut quickly if you are adept at cutting to a line—a guide is impractical—the circular saw is far simpler to use. For a bevel no sharper than 45 degrees, set a sliding bevel to the angle of the cut *(opposite, far left)* then unplug the saw, set its blade to the maximum cutting depth and lay it upside down. Hold the handle of the sliding bevel firmly against the bottom of the base plate, loosen the protractor nut on the blade-angle scale at the front of the saw, retract the saw guard and tilt the base plate until the blade of the sliding bevel lies flat against the saw blade. Tighten the protractor nut to secure the setting.

Mark a line square across the board and align the blade with it, using the guide at the front of the base plate. (Check the alignment of the blade and the line carefully by eye; many guides are imprecise.) Start the cut with the guard raised as described for angle cuts *(above, right)*.

For a bevel sharper than 45 degrees in carcassing timber, use a protractor to set the sliding bevel to the complement of the angle desired, then use the sliding bevel to set the saw blade as described above. For sharp bevels in shaped boards, such as finishes, use a mitre box *(overleaf)*.

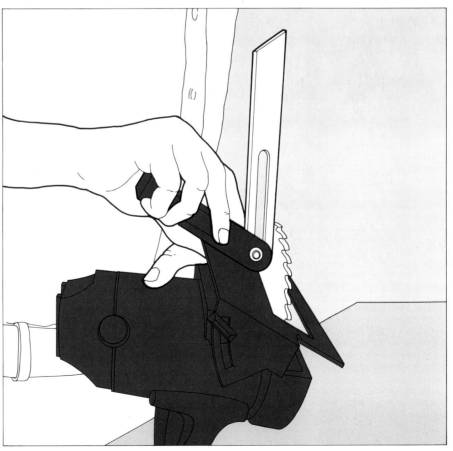

Making a compound cut. With a handsaw, this two-directional cut generally requires two separate operations—a simple angle cut followed by a bevel cut. With a circular saw it is done in a single pass. Mark the simple angle, then set the saw blade for the bevel *(page 27, bottom)*, but follow the cutting procedure that is used for a simple angle *(page 27, top right)*.

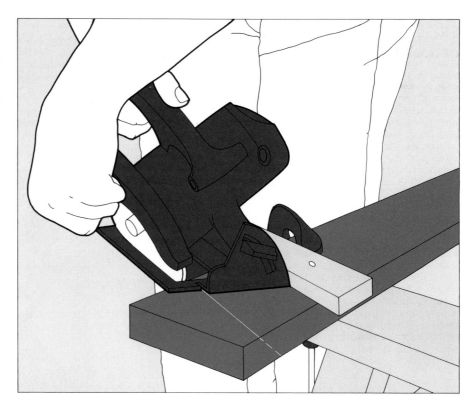

Cutting with a Mitre Box

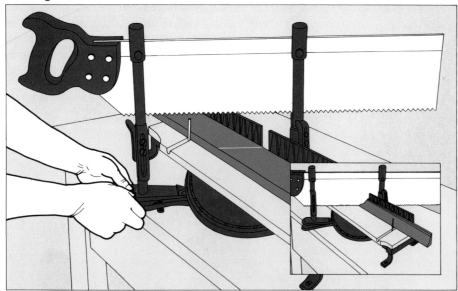

SCRAP WOOD

Making simple angle or bevel cuts. Set the saw angle desired, correcting for scale error if necessary. For a simple angle cut, place the board flat side down in the box and secure it in position—using either mitre-box cramps or woodworking cramps—so the saw will cut on the waste side of the mark. Lower the saw and make the cut.

Follow the same procedure for a bevel cut, but place the board on edge, with its flat side against the back of the mitre box *(inset)*.

Making a cut sharper than 45 degrees. Measure and mark the angle to be cut and place the marked board in the mitre box. Move the saw as close to the cutting line as possible, then shift the board to align the cutting line with the blade.

Fit a block of scrap wood between the back of the mitre box and the board and clamp the block in place. Hold the board firmly while you make the cut, checking constantly that the cutting line does not stray from the plane of the saw.

A Radial Arm Saw
for Speed and Precision

Setting the saw for simple angle cuts. For a right-hand angle cut, loosen the mitre lock and swing the arm to the right, setting the indicator on the mitre scale to the angle you will cut, correcting for scale error if necessary. On a typical radial arm saw, the arm will lock automatically at 45 degrees, and you must release the lock to move it. Mark the board and brace it against the fence with your left hand, positioning it so that the blade will cut on the waste side of the mark; use your right hand to pull the saw through the board. If precision is important, make a test cut on a scrap of wood.

To cut a left-hand mitre in a flat board, turn the board upside down and use the right-hand mitre position. If the board surface is shaped and will not lie flat when turned upside down, move the fence to its rear position and swing the saw to the left to lock it in the left-hand mitre position *(inset)*. Use a supplementary worktable if necessary, to support the wood, and pull the saw through the board with your left hand.

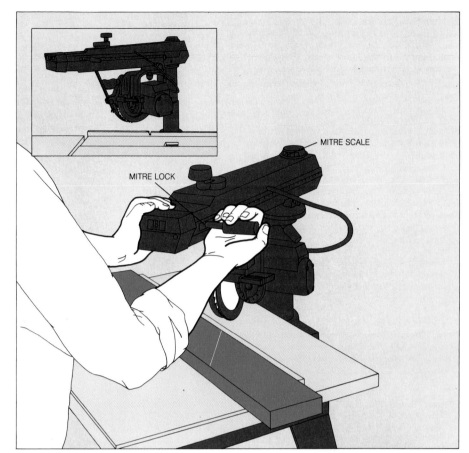

MITRE SCALE

MITRE LOCK

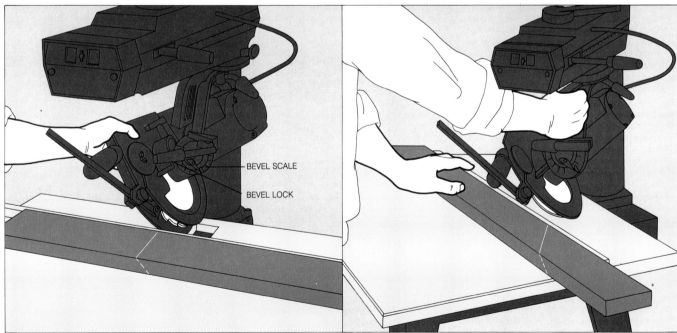

BEVEL SCALE

BEVEL LOCK

Making bevel and compound cuts. For a bevel cut, raise the arm of the saw until the blade clears the table by about 75 mm; release the bevel lock and tilt the blade anticlockwise to the correct degree reading on the bevel scale *(above)*, then retighten the lock. Make sure the guard has enough play so that it will not jam when you move the saw; if necessary, clear the guard of sawdust and lubricate it. (If the guard jams, stop the saw immediately and free the guard.) Use your right hand to position and steady the wood and your left hand to pull the saw. Make a test cut to check accuracy. For a compound cut, set both the mitre and the bevel scales. The cutting procedure follows that used for a bevel cut, but switch hand positions if the saw is set for a right-hand mitre *(above)*.

A Power Mitre Box
for Speedy Crosscuts

A handy hybrid. A cross between a mitre box *(pages 16 and 28)* and a radial arm saw *(pages 17 and 29)*, the power mitre box is the professional's tool of choice for making quick work of sawing a large number of mitre and bevel cuts. As with the radial arm saw, the blade spins down and away from the user, forcing the wood against the table and fence. Unlike the radial arm saw, however, the saw on this tool does not travel forwards and back on a horizontal arm; instead it pivots up and down on a fixed axis. The mitre box has a control arm to change the angle of the blade relative to the fence, plus a pointer on the arm to indicate the selected angle on a scale fitted to the front of the table.

In use, the screw can swing about 48 degrees right or left of a centre line, marked 0 degrees, perpendicular to the fence; on most models the blade automatically locks when it stops at positions of 0 degrees, 22.5 degrees, and 45 degrees. The saw handle, equipped with a trigger, controls the vertical movement of the blade. As the blade is lowered into the wood, the clear plastic blade guard rises and sawdust is carried from the work surface through a dust spout. The assembly is bolted to the table through holes in the base.

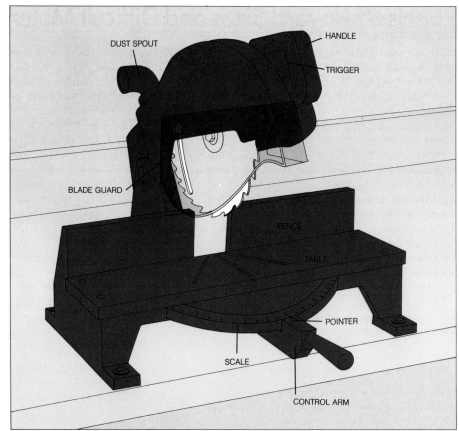

Making an angled cut. Using the control arm, set the blade to the proper angle, here 45 degrees to the right of the centre line. If the blade has not been automatically locked in place, secure it—usually with a latch or screw on the control arm. Align your body with the blade, and use one hand to hold the wood to be cut firmly against the fence, keeping your fingers clear of the blade area. Slide the wood along the table until the cutting line rests beneath the blade. Then grip the handle with your other hand, pull the trigger, and slowly and evenly pull the saw down. When the cut is made, raise the blade and release the trigger, but keep your hands in place until the blade comes to a complete stop.

Use either hand to grip the handle, depending on whether the cutting angle falls to the left or right side of the centre line. But never cross your hands in front of the saw to hold the wood against the fence, and never obscure your line of vision with the blade. Do not attempt to cut pieces shorter than 200 mm—the wood might fly from your hands. For long pieces, make outrigger supports of scrap wood to keep the far ends from sagging as you work.

Panels: Awkward Sizes and Difficult Materials

Much carpentry today requires the cutting of large, awkward panels. Flooring, roof decking and cupboards are now almost always constructed of plywood or chipboard, and it is also common practice to have interior doors covered with panels of either plywood or hardboard.

Panels are difficult to cut partly because of their size but also because of their composition. The glues and binders that hold together the veneer layers of plywood or the chopped-up wood in chipboard quickly dull saw blades.

The big problem, however, is size. To hold clumsily large pieces, you need a firm work surface; to make a long cut straight, you need a guide.

Two sturdy sawhorses alone provide support when crosscutting with a circular saw, but ripping requires additional stiffeners—two 100 by 50 mm boards that prevent the panel from sagging as the saw passes along the panel's midsection. With a radial arm saw, use two outrigger tables bolted to the floor; smooth tops reduce friction as the panels move past the blade. A third outrigger table helps when cutting many panels—it supports the waste piece and lets one person do the entire job.

Straightedge guides are equally important. You can make a guide for a circular saw, using the perfectly square factory-cut edge of a piece of chipboard. A two-piece, permanent jig is best for repeated crosscuts; a one-piece jig, assembled for a single job, is sufficient for ripping.

For smoothness as well as straightness of cut, the blade you choose is important. Standard rip and crosscut blades dull quickly. A carbide-tipped combination blade will stand up longer to the materials in plywood and chipboard, but it will give a relatively rough cut. A special plywood blade will give a cleaner, smoother cut but will dull faster than the carbide-tipped combination blade.

If you own a radial arm saw, use it for panel cutting when you can do the job conveniently in your workshop. The crosscutting capacity is limited by the length of the arm, but by cutting in two stages *(page 33, top)* you can cut widths of up to twice the arm length. You can rip widths from 350 to 600 mm with the saw in the out-rip position *(page 33, bottom)*. And if the piece to be ripped from the panel is wider than this, simply measure the piece you need, subtract that measurement plus the kerf width from the width of the panel and set the saw up for an in-rip cut *(pages 22 to 25)*.

A Home-Made Guide for Crosscuts

1 **Assembling the jig.** Screw together two 1200 mm lengths of 18 mm chipboard, one of the pieces 300 mm wide and the other 100 mm wide, cut from an end of the panel that has an unmarred factory-cut edge. Align the two pieces so that the factory-cut edge of the narrow piece faces into the middle of the wide piece.

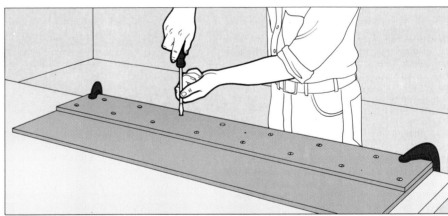

2 **Trimming the jig.** Clamp the jig to the bench top so that at least 150 mm of the wide board extends over the bench edge. Set the base plate of the saw against the factory-cut edge of the narrow piece, and saw through the wide piece along its entire length. The edge of the narrow piece thus becomes a guide to position the saw blade at the edge of the wide piece—the jig's cutting edge. Varnish the jig to reduce the warping.

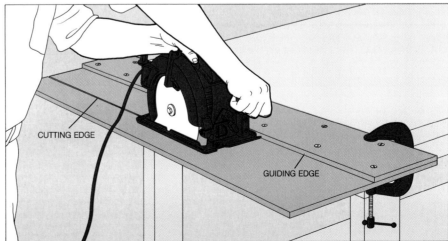

CUTTING EDGE

GUIDING EDGE

3 **Cutting the panel.** Align the cutting edge of the jig base with marks for the amount to be cut off. Clamp the jig to the panel and, using the cutting edge of the jig as a guide, score the panel with a utility knife or, to prevent gouging the jig, a chisel held bevel side out but tilted towards you.

Set the blade depth to allow for the thickness of the jig base as well as that of the panel to be cut, position the base plate against the guiding edge of the jig as in Step 2, and then saw through the panel, using the crosscutting technique described on page 14, Steps 1 and 2.

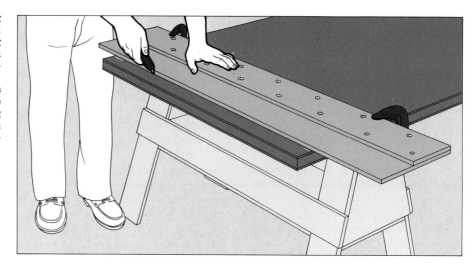

Making Clean Cuts with the Grain

1 **Building a work surface.** Set two sawhorses at a distance 600 mm shorter than the length of the panel to be cut. Nail two 100 by 50 mm boards as long as the panel to the sawhorses, keeping the boards parallel and about a metre apart.

2 **Positioning the jig.** Mark both panel ends for the amount to be cut off, make a second pair of marks further into the panel a distance equal to the distance between the saw blade and the base plate's left side; then clamp to the panel at the second pair of marks a piece of 18 mm chipboard 2440 mm long by 250 mm wide that has been cut to leave a factory-made edge as a base-plate guide. At three places along the midsection of this jig, check that the jig edge and panel edge are the same distance apart as at the ends; at these places nail the jig to the panel. Cut the panel following Step 3, above.

If the plywood panel has been previously cut, its edge may be bowed or out of square. In this case, measure from the factory-cut edge and use a string to check alignment of your jig.

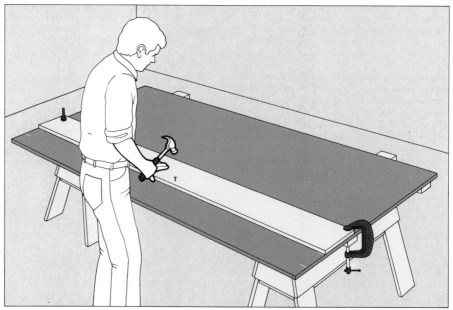

Cutting Panels with a Radial Arm Saw

A two-stage crosscut. Move the fence closer to the arm's support post by loosening the cramps behind the table and sliding the spacer boards towards you. Position the fence between the cramps and the spacer boards and tighten the cramps. Position the panel against the fence and proceed as for a normal crosscut *(page 18)* until the cut extends just over half way across the panel. Return the saw blade to its rest position behind the fence. Turn the board over and draw a pencil line from the inside edge of the kerf of the first cut to the uncut edge of the panel. Align the pencil mark exactly with the blade *(right)* and complete the panel crosscut.

If the surface appearance of the panel is important, the panel must be rotated horizontally after the first cut—rather than turned over—so that the same face remains uppermost for both cuts. The panel should also be rotated if the sides are not parallel; in this case, the panel should be clamped to the worktable after you have aligned the cut with the blade, rather than held against the fence.

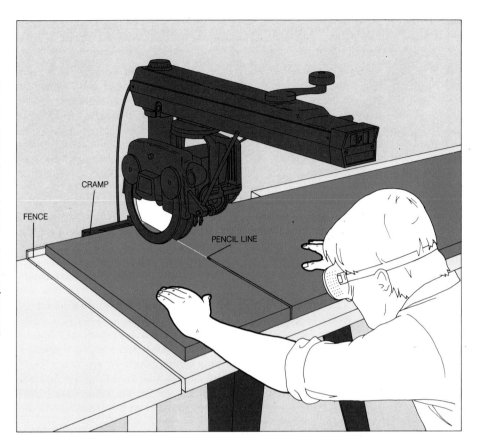

CRAMP

FENCE

PENCIL LINE

Making long rip cuts. With the fence in the back position *(above)*, turn the saw to the out-rip position (blade parallel to the fence, motor between blade and fence). Set the panel to the left of the saw with the leading edge against the fence, align the blade with the cutting line on the panel end and lock the motor in place. Adjust the blade guard and antikickback fingers *(page 24)*, start the motor and, with your left hand on the back of the panel and your right hand keeping pressure against the fence, feed the panel into the blade.

If you are working with a helper, do not let him take hold of the waste piece until it is two-thirds of the way past the blade; from that point on, let him merely support the wood and not pull it. Finish the cut as you would for in-ripping *(page 25, Step 5)*.

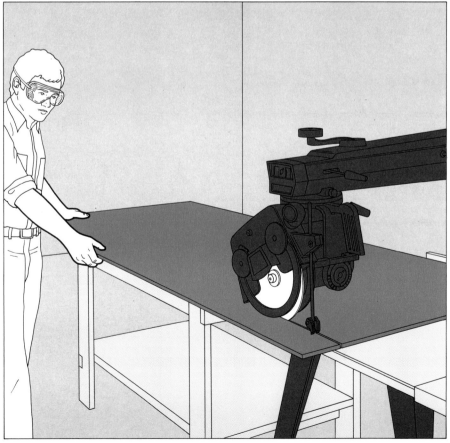

The Tricks of Putting Curves into Wood

The structural timbers of a house fit together along straight lines, but much of the finish carpentry involves curves, trickier to cut. Some curved cuts are utilitarian—for example, in holes through floors and ceilings for pipes or ducts. Others—the scalloped trim of a porch or the curve of a circular window—are decorative.

Whatever the curve's purpose, it requires tools and techniques different from those used for straight cuts. For most curves the best tool is an electric jigsaw, ideally one with variable speed control. Blades 6 mm wide with 8 to 10 points per 25 mm are suitable for most jobs, but other blades are available for special uses: a fine blade with more than 12 teeth per 25 mm will make splinter-free cuts in plywood; a narrower blade with 12 or 14 teeth per 25 mm is advisable for scrollwork.

When power is not available or when work space is too cramped for a jigsaw, turn to any of several handsaws designed specifically for cutting curves. A coping saw has a delicate blade and a limited cutting range; it is best suited to finish joints in woodwork and to fine, intricate scroll-work. The keyhole saw can tackle heavier tasks, while the compass saw serves for still rougher work. Both come with an assortment of blades designed for different materials. The blades are tapered, with narrow tips for turns and for cutouts started from small drilled holes; and because the blades can be reversed, compass and keyhole saws are ideal for use in jobs with tight clearances and awkward undercuts.

Since you must guide all of these saws freehand, it is essential to mark a guideline before cutting any curve. More often than not, you can simply hold an object to be duplicated—a section of a decorative architrave, perhaps—in place and trace its outline. But some situations demand more complex calculations and marking techniques. For instance, to mark an elliptical hole for a round pipe passing through a sloping ceiling you must plot the pitch of the ceiling and the size of the pipe on cardboard, then cut out the marked cardboard as a template to transfer the ellipse to the ceiling *(pages 37–38)*.

In other situations you must resort to scribing, a marking technique for fitting material to an existing curve. Usually it consists of setting the wood—the floorboards in a semicircular alcove, for instance—against the curve and running a simple school compass round the curve to duplicate, or scribe, the arc on the boards *(page 35)*. If you are scribing overlapping boards, as when you fit cladding round a circular opening *(page 36)*, you must position the work carefully and set the compass to the exact distance that will provide the overlap. And for some jobs, such as the cutting of a curved architrave for an archway, you will have to combine template-making and scribing.

When you cut a curve, be especially careful of the pressure you apply; under excess pressure, a handsaw blade will buckle and a jigsaw blade may shoot out of the cut or snap in two. Mark the guidelines for a jigsaw on the unfinished side of the board if possible, because the upstroke cut of the blade splinters the wood; if you must work on the finished side, cover the guidelines with transparent tape to minimize the damage. Steady the board by clamping it to a worktable or setting it on sawhorses.

Sawing an Irregular Outline

Cutting an interior curve with a handsaw. Drill a starter hole through the waste area, insert the tip of the saw blade—in this example, a compass saw—and make a few short vertical strokes to start the cut. Then lower the blade to a 45 degree angle and follow the curved guideline with long, even strokes and light pressure—too much pressure on the blade will bend or buckle it. To saw round sharp turns, use short strokes, made with the narrow tip of the blade.

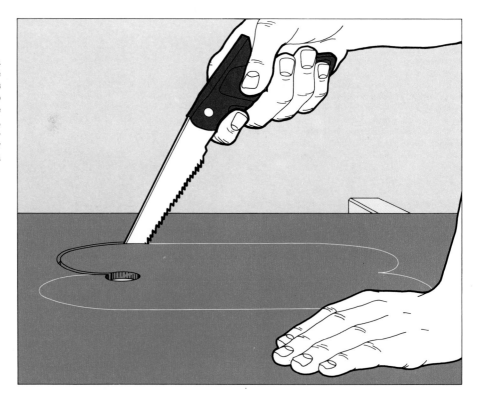

Cutting with a jigsaw. Pressing the saw down and forwards and keeping the base plate flat against the wood, follow the broad curves of a pattern. Bypass any sharp turns, forcing the saw or pushing it sideways, for these curves will damage the blade. When you have cut the waste wood away from the broad curves, go back to the sharper angles. On a tight curve, where the saw blade is likely to bind, make radial cuts in the waste area, then saw along the outline. The waste will drop off in pieces as you saw, giving the blade more room to turn *(inset)*.

A plunge cut for an interior curve. With the saw motor off and the blade clear of the wood, rest the front edge, or toe, of the base plate on the waste area near the marked guideline. Turn the motor on and, pressing firmly on the base-plate toe, slowly lower the back of the saw until the blade touches and cuts through the wood. When the base plate rests flat on the wood, saw to the guideline and cut in the normal fashion.

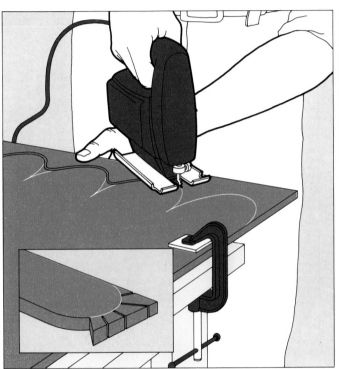

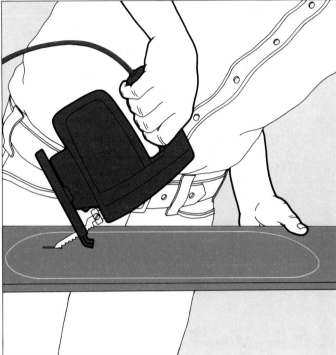

Scribing a Gentle Arc

Copying a curve with a compass. Butt the material against the curve it must fit—in this example, the material is floorboards, the curve is that of an alcove wall—and set the legs of a compass to a distance slightly greater than the widest gap between the curve and the edges of the boards. Keeping the plane of the legs at a right angle to the surface you are marking, and in a line that remains parallel with the boards, move the compass points round the curve so the pencil point marks a corresponding curve on the boards.

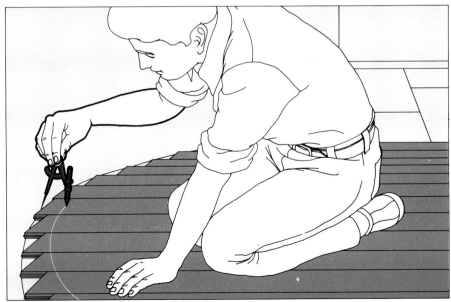

Fitting Cladding to a Curve

1 The bottom board. To fit a feather-edged or overlap boarding round the curve of a circular window frame, you must scribe and cut a series of arcs on the boards. Tack the first board to be cut directly over the last complete board below the frame, add the width of the board overlap to the distance between the bottom of the frame and the top of the tacked board, and subtract the total from the width of the board. Set the legs of a compass to this distance and use the compass to scribe an arc on the tacked board. Take the marked board down, cut the curve and install the board at the bottom of the frame.

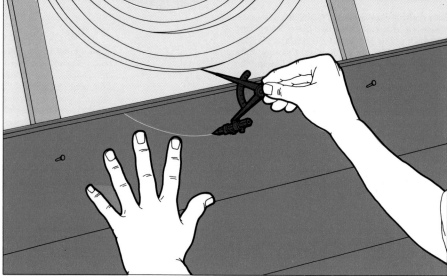

2 The side boards. Tack a side board at its correct level and about 50 mm from the frame, set the legs of a compass as you would for simple scribing *(page 35)*, and scribe the arc on the board. Mark, cut and install all the side boards before starting the final step of the job.

3 The top board. Above the frame, tack a board perfectly level, with its bottom edge resting on the frame. Set the compass legs to the width of the board overlap plus the gap between the last side board and the tacked board, and move the compass point along the top of the frame to scribe the final arc.

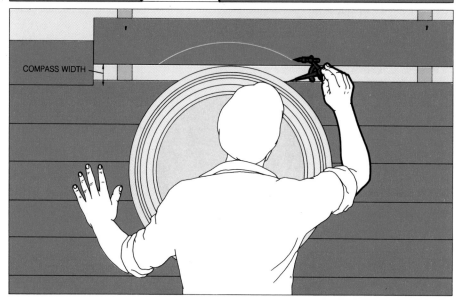

COMPASS WIDTH

How to Mark an Ellipse

1 **Finding the axes.** To plan an elliptical hole for a cylinder passing through a sloping plane—typically, a cylindrical vent or flue passing through a sloping ceiling—first find the axes of the ellipse by the following method. On a large piece of cardboard, draw a horizontal and a sloped line at the exact angle of the pitch. In any section of the horizontal line, mark off the diameter of the pipe plus any required clearance; then draw perpendicular lines from the marks to intersect the sloped line.

From the intersection points, extend two more lines perpendicular to the sloped line, mark off the pipe diameter plus clearance on these lines, and connect the marks to form a rectangle with its base on the sloped line. Finally, draw two lines bisecting the four sides of the rectangle. The longer line is the major axis of the ellipse; the shorter one is the minor axis.

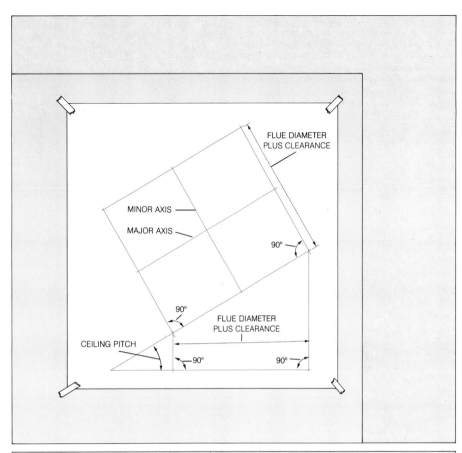

2 **Finding the focuses.** Set the legs of a compass to half the length of the major axis; place the point of the compass at either end of the minor axis and swing the pencil in an arc that intersects the major axis at two points. These points are the focuses of the ellipse.

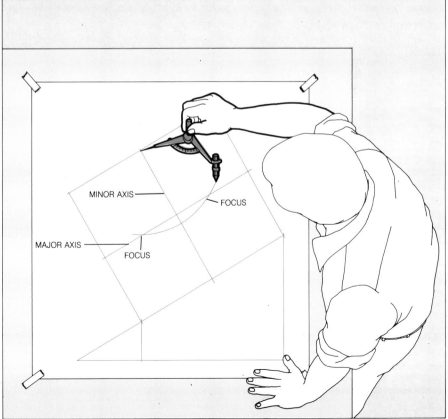

3 **Drawing the ellipse.** Set the cardboard on a piece of scrap wood and drive nails part way into the wood through the focuses and at one end of the minor axis. Tie a string tightly around the three nails; then replace the nail on the axis with a pencil and, keeping the string taut, swing the pencil round to outline the ellipse. Cut out the cardboard ellipse as a template for transferring the curve to the roof.

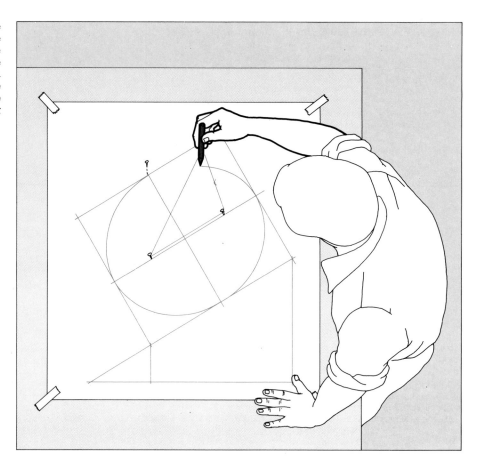

Tracing an Archway

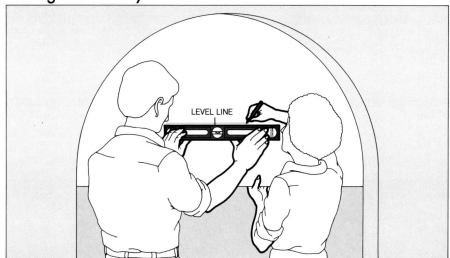

1 **Transferring the curve to paper.** To cut a large arc from straight boards, as in the architrave for an arched doorway or window opening, it is necessary to make a set of templates. First, tape a piece of paper over the arc and outline the entire curve on the paper. Have a helper hold a spirit level against the paper within 600 mm of the top of the arc, and mark a level line across the paper.

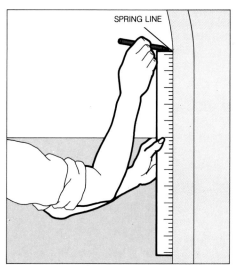

2 **Finding the spring line.** If the curved part of the architrave joins a straight section, as in an arch, move a straightedge up and down against the straight section and mark the paper at the highest spot where no space can be seen between the straightedge and the straight section. This marks the spring line, where the curve of the arc begins. Mark the spring line on the other side of the arch, then lay the paper on the floor.

3 **Scribing the template.** Set the legs of a compass to the width of the pieces you will cut—generally, the architrave width—and run the point along the marked arc to scribe a second arc above it. From the centre of the level, draw a perpendicular line up through the double arc.

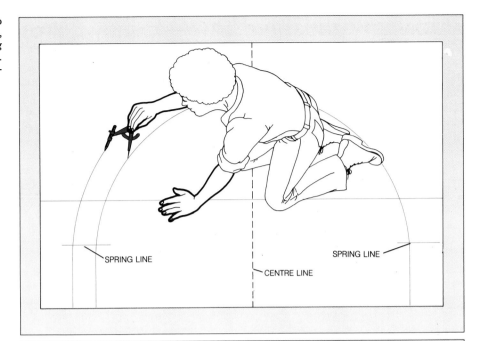

SPRING LINE

SPRING LINE

CENTRE LINE

4 **Dividing the template.** At the top of the double arc, draw a line perpendicular to the centre line and parallel to the level line below. Along this top line, set the top edge of the board you will cut; on the template paper draw a line along the bottom edge of the board to intersect the double arc on both sides. This second line marks the divisions between the top and side templates.

To complete the side templates, draw lines across the double arc about 125 mm below each of the spring lines and parallel to the level line. These lines mark the butt joints at the bottoms of the two side templates. Cut the paper at both curves, at the division lines and at the butt joints, making three sections. Tack them to boards *(inset)*, and then trace their outlines as your guidelines.

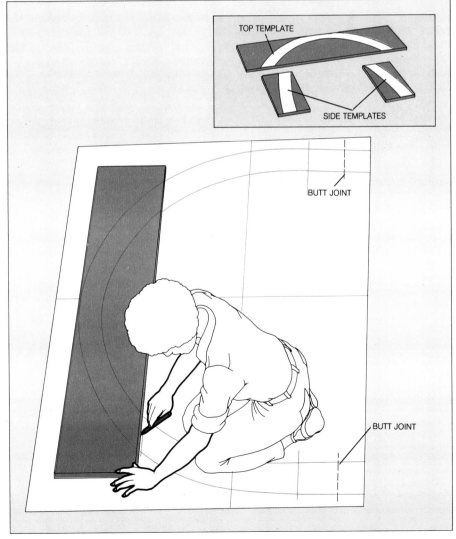

TOP TEMPLATE

SIDE TEMPLATES

BUTT JOINT

BUTT JOINT

Table Saw and Band Saw—Handy Extras

House carpentry rarely calls for fixed power tools—the radial arm saw is the only one that is discussed in detail in this chapter. But two other types of fixed saw, the bench saw and the band saw, can be very useful in home workshops. Neither of these offers the combination of versatility and accuracy that distinguishes the radial arm saw; but if you have either tool, you may want to consider using it for some cutting jobs.

A bench saw consists essentially of a power-driven circular blade that projects through a slot in a metal worktable (the safety guard that always covers the blade and the riving knife, which prevents the timber binding on the back of the blade, have been omitted for clarity in the pictures below and opposite, top). The saw has an adjustable rip fence and a completely unobstructed space around its blade so that it can make rip cuts in long boards. However, because the wood must be moved past the blade, large panels are troublesome to handle. A second fence, which is set at an angle to the blade with a mitre gauge, is used to push boards past the blade for crosscuts and mitre cuts, and a crank or lever tilts the blade for bevel cuts.

On the band saw, the blade is exactly what the name implies—a continuous steel band. It runs in tracks on an upper and a lower wheel, and is covered at the wheels by guards and at the rear of the saw by a throat, or vertical arm, so that only the section above the worktable is exposed. Using a thin, flexible blade—as narrow as 3 mm—you can pivot the wood freehand for precise curves. With stronger, wider blades—the maximum width is generally 37 mm—you can take advantage of the saw's great depth of cut (up to 150 mm on the majority of models) to make straight cuts on very thick timber or to slice a thick board into several thinner ones.

Both types of saw call for careful planning and adjustments. On the bench saw, you must adjust the blade height so that the teeth will protrude about 3 mm above the surface of the wood you are cutting. For an accurate rip cut, you must set the rip fence to an exact distance from the blade (if the tips of the saw teeth are alternately slanted left and right, measure from a tooth that slants in the direction of the fence).

For an angle cut you will need to slide the mitre gauge into a slot to the left or right of the blade (carpenters prefer the left slot for the majority of cuts), set the gauge to the desired angle, mark an exact guideline on the board and use a mitre-gauge extension—a straight piece of wood that screws or bolts to the gauge—to hold the board steady while the cut is made. For cutting wide boards and panels, table extensions and a helper are generally necessary.

The band saw has special problems of control. Because you need to guide the board freehand for curved cuts, be sure to mark guidelines that are especially accurate. And because the throat of the saw can obstruct the movement of the board in the course of a long curve, you must plan your starting point and your movements with care—for certain cuts, the best strategy is to lay out the cutting lines on both faces of the board and turn the board over in mid-cut.

With both saws, take the general safety precautions that apply to all power tools—and for a bench saw add a few special ones. Stand to the side of the blade—if it binds, the board may shoot backwards. Use a push stick to feed the board for a narrow rip cut *(page 25, bottom, centre)*, and insert a wedge in the kerf of any rip cut that is more than a metre long, to prevent the blade from binding *(page 21, top)*.

Other workshop tools such as the overhead planer come in handy for occasional jobs. One home-made tool—a sturdy sawhorse *(pages 42–43)*—is almost a necessity.

Making Straight Cuts with a Table Saw

Ripping a board. Turn the saw on, press the board lightly against the fence with your left hand and hook the last two fingers of your right hand over the fence; use the first two fingers and thumb to push the board towards the blade, and remove your left hand at least 150 mm before the end of the cut. If the distance between the rip fence and the board is 150 mm or more, complete the cut with your right hand, bringing the hand back in a high arc above the table; if the distance between fence and board is less than 150 mm use a stick to push the work past the blade.

Some boards can be allowed to slide off the far end of the table after the cut is made. For boards longer than 600 mm, however, get a helper to ease the board off the table; for wide panels, station another helper at the left of the table to keep the panel flush against the fence.

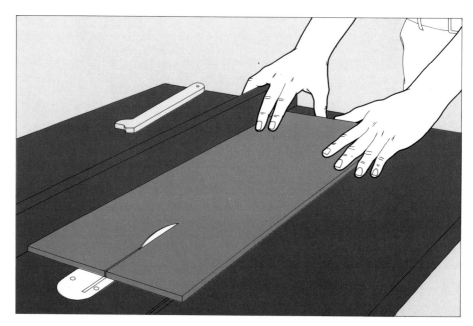

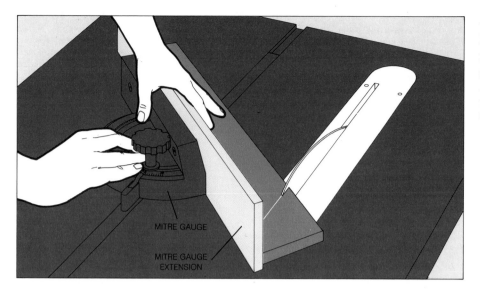

A mitre cut. Set the mitre gauge, fitted with a smooth wood extension, to the desired angle, then hold the board against the extension with your left hand and, with your right, push the gauge forwards. The blade will tend to pull the board off course during the cut; take care to keep the cutting line on the board aligned with the blade by using firm forward pressure and holding the board tight against the gauge extension.

Cutting Curves with a Band Saw

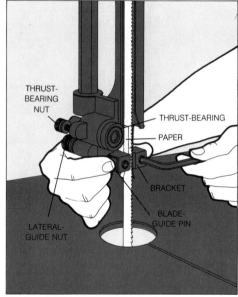

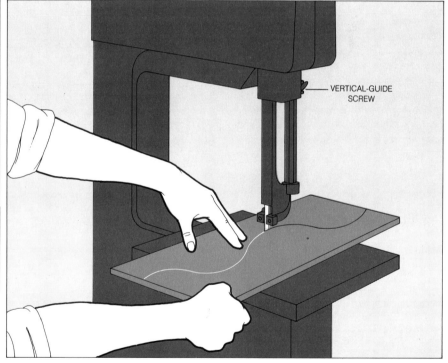

1 Adjusting the blade support and guides. After putting a new blade in place, turn the thrust-bearing adjustment nut so that the thrust-bearing is as close as possible to the back of the blade without touching it. Use the lateral-guide nut to set the edges of the guide-pin brackets flush with the gullets between the teeth of the blade. To adjust the clearance between the guide pins and the blade, loosen the brackets with an allen key, wrap a piece of heavy paper round the blade— brown wrapping paper will do—and press the guide pins together against the paper; then tighten the brackets and remove the paper.

2 Making the cut. Set the blade guides to a distance of 6 mm above the board with the vertical-guide screw, then turn on the saw; feed the board into the blade with your right hand and turn the board with your left to keep the blade on the guideline. Cut at a steady pace—if you stop or move the board too slowly, the blade will burn the wood. At all times, keep both hands well away from the blade; hook the fingers of your right hand over the near edge of the board and move the left hand back whenever it gets within 100 mm of the blade. As you finish the cut, your hands will necessarily draw close to the blade:

take care to keep your fingers clear of it. Pull your hands back by moving them in wide arcs to each side of the blade; turn off the saw and wait until the blade has stopped completely.

When a turn is so sharp that the blade tends to bind, do not increase your feeding pressure. If you have reached a point close to the edge of the board, run the blade out of the board through the waste area, then cut back in from another angle. If you have just begun the cut, turn off the motor, backtrack through the cut, and reposition the board so that you can approach the curve from another direction.

The Necessity: a Solid Sawhorse:

Making a sawhorse is a traditional test of a carpenter's skill. Construction foremen sometimes ask a new man to build a sawhorse from scratch—and hire him or not, according to the quality of his work. Unlike most tests of skill, the job produces something useful, for a sawhorse is an essential tool in working with wood, and good ones cannot be bought ready-made. The ones sold as kits, to be assembled with metal brackets, are not as desirable as hand-made ones because their brackets can damage saw blades and they are not sturdy enough.

The home-made sawhorse illustrated here resists tipping, is rigid enough to support almost any load and wide enough to stand on comfortably. Its braced shelf stores tools, a wide top serves as a portable workbench, and strong side pieces make a low scaffold, complete with built-in steps. For general work, most sawhorses have more or less standard dimensions: a length of 1 metre to support 2440 by 1220 mm sheets of plywood; a height of 600 mm, to hold work just above knee height for easy sawing; and a width at the base of 350 mm.

A standard sawhorse. The 100 by 25 mm legs of this sawhorse, splayed for stability and braced by plywood end pieces, fit snugly into angled notches in the 100 by 50 mm top; a 225 by 25 mm shelf, notched for the legs, fits tightly beneath the end pieces. Raised 50 by 25 mm side braces keep tools from rolling off the shelf and serve as steps when the sawhorse is used as a scaffold; 50 by 25 mm cross-braces beneath the shelf provide extra support and stability.

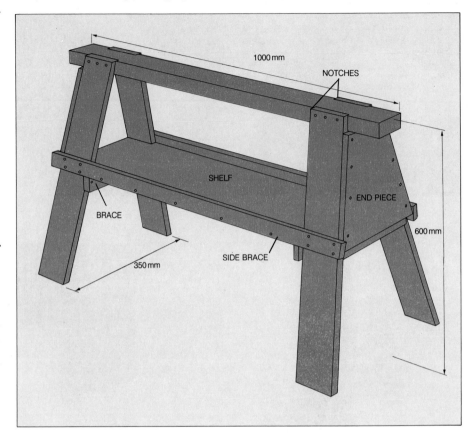

Putting the Pieces Together

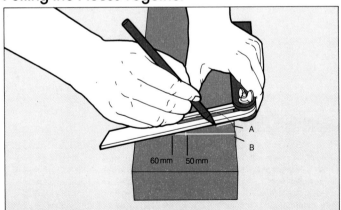

1 Setting the angles. On a scrap of wood, mark A and B 10 mm apart. Use a combination square to draw a line from point B across the wood at right angles to the side. Mark two points on this line 50 and 60 mm from point B. Butt the stock of the bevel along the side, align the blade between point A and the 60 mm mark, and tighten the wing nut to set a 1:6 angle. For a 1:5 angle, align the blade between point A and the 50 mm mark.

2 Marking the legs. With the bevel at a 1:6 angle, draw a line at least 10 mm from the end of a 100 by 25 mm board. Draw a line parallel to this one 630 mm along the board. Turn the board on its side and set the bevel at a 1:5 angle. Align the blade with the mark on the board face and draw a line across the edge *(inset)*. Repeat at the other end. Cut the board and use as a template for the other legs.

3 **Fitting the legs to the top.** Draw a line across a 1000 mm long, 100 by 50 mm board, 100 mm from one end. Set a sliding bevel to a 1:6 angle, hold it on the edge of the board at the end of the marked line and slanting out towards the end of the board, and draw a line along its blade. To determine the width of the notch, set a leg against the angled line and draw a line along the other side of the leg; from this line, draw a square line across the 100 by 50 mm board *(inset)* and draw matching lines on the other edge with a bevel. Mark the other end in the same way.

4 **Marking the depth of the notches.** Set a marking gauge *(page 20, bottom right)* at 9 mm and score the top of the 100 by 50 mm board on each side between the square lines (the bottom of the notch will meet the edge). Saw along the angled lines and chisel out the waste between saw cuts *(inset)*. Lay out and cut the notches at the other end of the 100 by 50 mm board, then fasten each leg into a notch with three No. 8, 37 mm nails.

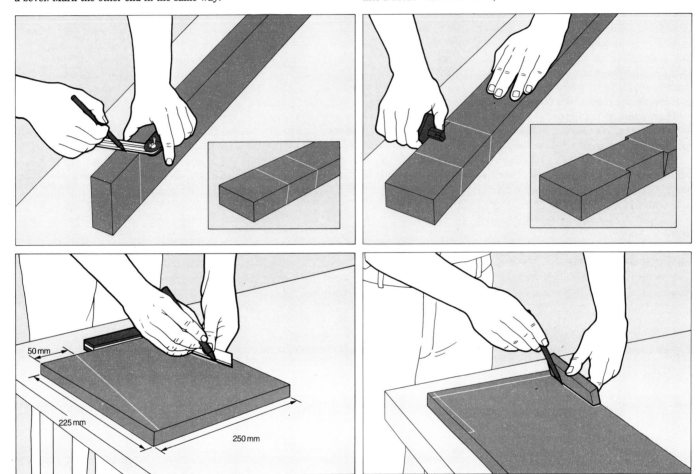

5 **Marking the ends.** Cut two pieces of 18 mm plywood, 250 by 225 mm. On one piece, mark a point 50 mm in from the end of one 250 mm side. Using a sliding bevel set at a 1:5 angle and a straight-edge, draw a line down from the 50 mm mark until it meets the opposite side. Mark a point 145 mm on from the 50 mm point, turn the bevel over and draw a second line to the opposite side. Cut along the two lines, and use the trapezium shape as a template to cut a matching end piece from the other sheet of plywood. Secure the end pieces to the legs, positioning them beneath the top, with No. 8, 37 mm nails.

6 **Adding a shelf.** From a 25 mm sheet of plywood, cut out a piece to fit just below the end pieces and across the overall width of the legs. Lay out notches for the legs by drawing a line 19 mm from each end. At each corner of the shelf, hold an angled scrap—left over from cutting the legs *(Step 1)*—against the line and edge of the board, and trace round it. Cut within this outline with a handsaw, try the shelf for fit and pare the notches with a chisel. Nail the shelf in position.

Cut two 50 by 25 mm boards the length of the shelf. Hold each side piece against the sawhorse, flush with the bottom of the shelf—plane away the shelf's edge if necessary—and nail it to the shelf and legs. Cut two 50 by 25 mm braces to fit under the shelf and nail them across the legs.

Traditional Techniques of Saw-Sharpening

Using a saw with a dull blade mars the work and damages the tool. The blade cuts slowly and leaves rough edges; the added force needed to push the blade and keep it on course can buckle a handsaw or overheat a power saw until the metal cracks or the teeth break. On a power saw, a dull, overheated blade can scorch the wood and ruin the motor.

It makes sense, then, to check your saws for sharpness from time to time. Run your thumb lightly over the tops of the teeth; sharp teeth will prick your skin, but your thumb will slide over dull ones. On a handsaw, visually compare the teeth near the handle—which are rarely used—with teeth at the middle of the blade: worn teeth have rounded points; sharp teeth, angled points.

Some blades, particularly those on circular saws, are so inexpensive that they are more easily replaced then resharpened.

Others must be left to a professional: only a professional saw filer's specialized equipment can sharpen a carbide-tipped blade or restore a misshapen circular-saw blade.

But you can resharpen a handsaw or an ordinary circular saw blade yourself, by simply clamping the blade and touching up the edges of the teeth with a file. For handsaws, use a double-ended saw file; for circular blades, use a flat mill file. Handsaws can be clamped between long blocks of wood in a vice; to keep a circular blade stable while it is being filed, however, you will need to make a special jig that can hold blades of different diameters *(page 49)*.

On a handsaw, you can go beyond sharpening to master a craftsman's techniques for completely recutting a badly worn saw *(page 46)*. To begin with, you "joint" the saw—that is, file the tips of the teeth flat, to a uniform height. With another file you

reshape the flattened teeth; then, with a plier-like tool called a saw set, you bend them alternately to the right and to the left. Finally, you sharpen the saw as you would in retouching. Total recutting is an intricate job, in which every step must be performed with special precision. You may have difficulty locating professionals who perform this work properly, but with practice on an inexpensive blade, you can train yourself to meet the high standards of the old-time saw sharpener.

Start any job on a saw blade by checking the teeth for accumulations of resin and sap, which can clog a file. If necessary, clean the teeth by soaking the blade overnight in paraffin, then scrubbing it gently with a wire brush. To reduce the need for cleaning, use blades coated with a nonsticking plastic, or oil your steel blades lightly after each use.

Designs for Cutting

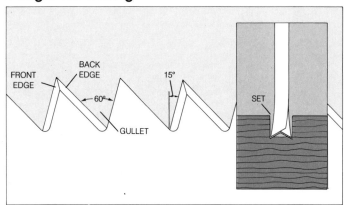

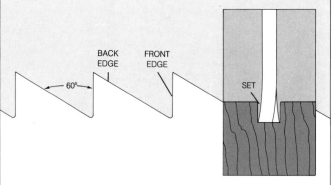

A crosscut handsaw. On each tooth, two bevelled edges meet at a sharp point. The front edge of a tooth is angled 15 degrees from the perpendicular and meets the back edge of the next tooth at a 60 degree angle; the valley between two teeth is a gullet. The teeth are bent, or set, alternately left and right of the blade, and each tooth is bevelled in the opposite direction of its set.

As you saw, the points of the set teeth score parallel grooves across the wood grain; then, on both the forward and return strokes, the bevelled edges of the teeth slice through the wood fibres between the grooves *(inset)*. Because the grooves are further apart than the thickness of the blade, the saw cuts a kerf that is wider than its blade, and is therefore unlikely to bind.

A ripsaw. The unbevelled edges of each tooth meet at the point in a chisel-like cutting edge. The gullets form 60 degree angles, like those of a crosscut saw, but the front edge is perpendicular to a line along the tops of the teeth.

A ripsaw tooth cuts like a tiny chisel, paring away wood on each forward stroke. The set *(inset)* may be greater than that of a crosscut saw, cutting wood faster but leaving it rougher.

Two circular blades. On a typical combination blade *(below, left)*, designed for ordinary crosscuts and rip cuts, the top of each tooth and part of each front edge are filed to form a sharp point; the backs of the teeth are unfiled. The bevel angles of the filed edges vary from one manufacturer to another, but the bevel of each tooth always slants away from the direction of its set. A blade designed to cut plywood is similar to this blade, but has smaller teeth.

The circular ripsaw blade *(below, right)* looks similar to the combination blade, but it has deeper gullets and less chunky teeth. Like a hand ripsaw, the teeth are unbevelled. The deep gullets give fast chip clearance.

A crosscut circular blade has teeth just like those of a crosscut handsaw *(opposite page, bottom left)*. These blades are much finer than a combination or ripsaw blade—often having 100 or more teeth as compared to 20 or 30 for the other two—and take much longer to sharpen.

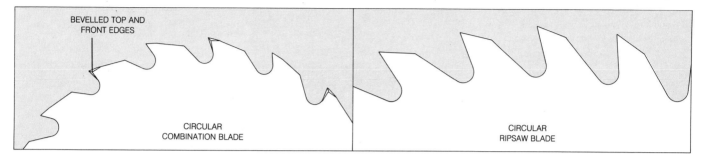

CIRCULAR
COMBINATION BLADE

CIRCULAR
RIPSAW BLADE

Files for Saws

Points per 25 mm	File
5–5½	175 mm
6	175 mm
7–8	150 mm
9–10	125 or 150 mm
11–12	100 or 110 mm

Choosing the right file. The left-hand column of this chart lists handsaw sizes according to the number of tooth points per 25 mm of saw blade; the right-hand column lists the corresponding sizes of triangular double-ended saw files for sharpening the saws. Manufacturers generally stamp the saw size on the blade near the handle; if you do not find it there, set a ruler just under the saw teeth, with a centimetre mark directly below a tooth point, and count the number of points in 25 mm, including the two points right above the marks.

Sharpening a Handsaw

Touching up the teeth. Secure the saw between blocks of wood in a vice, with the handle of the saw to your right and the gullets 6 mm above the wood blocks. At the handle end, place the file in the gullet in front of the first tooth set towards you. On a crosscut saw, like the one shown here, set the file in the gullet at an angle of 15 degrees from the horizontal, swing it to the left to a 60 degree angle with the blade, and rotate it about 15 degrees anticlockwise. Push the file forwards with a light, even pressure, lift the file from the gullet, and repeat the forward strokes until the bevelled edges on each side of the gullet are shiny. Use the same number of strokes for every second gullet along the blade.

Reverse the saw in the vice and follow the steps above, but swing the file to the right and rotate it clockwise for each stroke (whatever the saw position, point the file towards the handle).

File a ripsaw with the method for a crosscut saw, but keep the file horizontal and perpendicular to the blade, and rotate it 30 degrees.

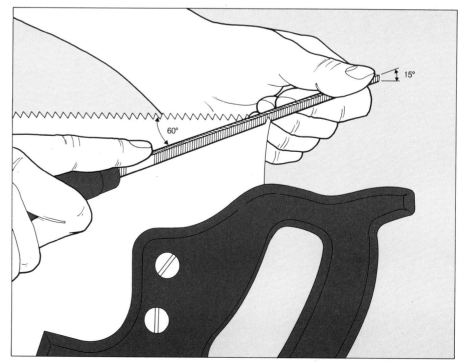

Recutting a Handsaw

1 Jointing the teeth. Secure the saw between blocks of wood in a vice, with the teeth about 50 mm above the wood blocks. Use a G-cramp to fasten a flat file to a small wood block, with half the width of the file extending beyond the edge of the block. Holding the block flat against the saw blade so that the file rests lightly on the tops of the saw teeth, run the file in forward strokes from the heel to the tip of the saw until each tooth has a small flat dot at the point; one or two strokes are usually sufficient.

If you find it hard to keep the block flat against the blade or the file flat on the teeth, use a manufactured hand jointer to secure the file *(inset, right)*.

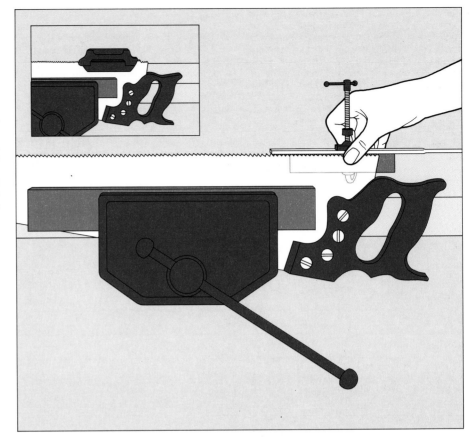

2 Shaping the teeth. Secure the saw as you would for touching up and choose the appropriate triangular double-ended file *(page 45, centre)*. On ripsaws, and on crosscut saws with teeth that accept a file in the touching-up position, use the procedures for touching up.

On a crosscut saw with teeth so flattened or misshapen that you cannot position the file for touching up, place the file in the front gullet of the first tooth that is set towards you, holding the file horizontal and perpendicular to the saw blade. Rotate the file 15 degrees anticlockwise and file straight across the blade, using pushing strokes only, until the gullet conforms to the shape of the file. Shape every alternate gullet in this way, then reverse the saw and the rotation of the file to shape the other gullets.

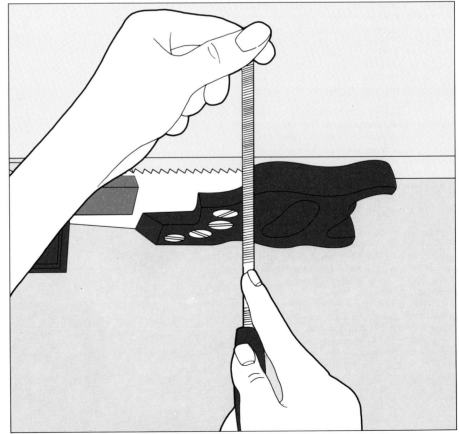

3 **Setting the saw.** Secure the saw, with the blade about 50 mm above the wood blocks in the vice. At the heel of the saw, position the first tooth that is set away from you between the anvil and the plunger of a saw set *(inset)*. This tooth is normally unworn, and does not need resetting; therefore, set the stop-adjusting and anvil-adjusting screws of the saw set so that when you close the handles tightly, the anvil and the plunger pinch the tooth without bending it. (Do not rely on adjusting-screw markings for different saw sizes; make your judgment by eye and feel.) Apply the saw set to every alternate tooth along the saw, squeezing the handles each time; reverse the saw to set the other teeth.

Complete the refitting job by touching up the edges of the teeth. This final touching up is necessary after resetting, even if the teeth were touched up as part of Step 2.

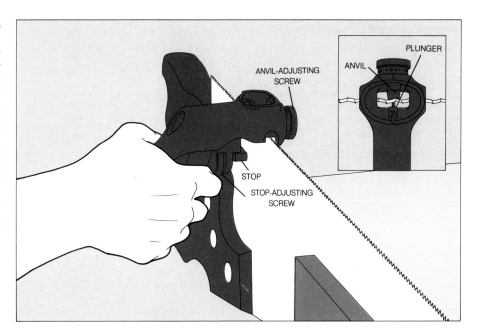

Touching Up a Ripsaw Circular-Saw Blade

Filing straight across. Secure the blade in a jig *(page 49)* clamped in a vice. Align the gullet of the first tooth to be sharpened with the pencil line on top of the jig. Using a flat mill file held horizontally and at right angles to the face of the blade, file the front of the tooth with forward strokes only *(right)*. File until the tooth front is shiny, but do not use more than four strokes. Set the face of the file on the top of the tooth and, keeping the file at the same angle, file the top in the same way.

To bring the next tooth to the top of the jig, set the file sideways into its gullet and pull it to align with the pencil mark on the jig. File each tooth with the same number of strokes. Because the teeth of a ripsaw blade are not bevelled, they can be sharpened from one side and there is no need to reverse the blade in the jig.

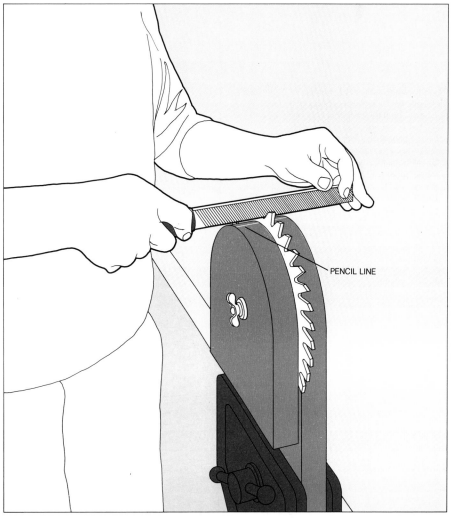

Touching up a Combination Circular-Saw Blade

1 **Filing the top edges.** Secure the blade in the jig and align the gullet of the first tooth set away from you with the pencil line marked on top of the jig. Lay the blade of a flat mill file over the bevel of the top edge of the tooth, and swing the handle until the face of the file lies flat against the bevel—you will usually have to move the file about 10 degrees out of square and downwards. File with forward strokes only until the bevel is shiny, using no more than four strokes.

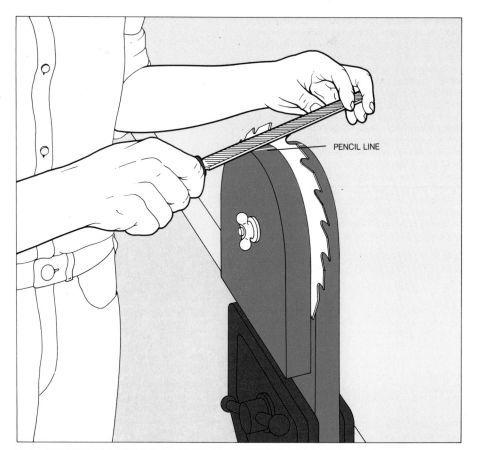

PENCIL LINE

2 **Filing the front edges.** Set the file sideways into the gullet with its face against the front bevel of the tooth. File this edge as in Step 1 to form a sharp point at the tip of the tooth.

Hook the file into the gullet of the next tooth set away from you and pull it to the top of the jig. Sharpen the edges of all the teeth set away from you with the same number of strokes per tooth; then turn the blade round in the jig and sharpen the other teeth in the same way.

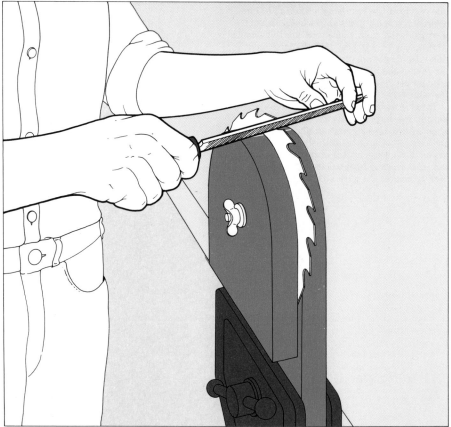

Making a Jig for a Circular-Saw Blade

1 Attaching the hinge. Cut two pieces of 19 mm blockboard or plywood 360 mm long and 180 mm wide, and use a jigsaw to shape one end of both pieces into a semicircle *(page 35)*. From the square end of one of the pieces, saw off a 120 mm section. Position one leaf of a 63 mm butt hinge on the shorter board so that the knuckle is centred along the straight edge. Use a bradawl to make starter holes and then screw the hinge leaf to the shorter board *(below)*.

2 Joining the boards. Turn over the shorter board and place it on the longer board, carefully aligning the semicircular ends. Pencil a line along the base of the hinge to mark its position on the longer board. Lift the shorter board and align the base of the hinge with the pencil mark. Holding the hinge down firmly with one hand, make starter holes with a bradawl and screw the hinge to the longer board *(below)*.

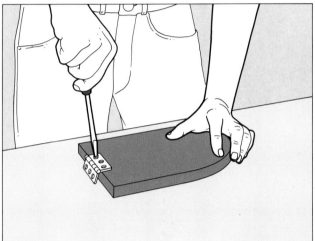

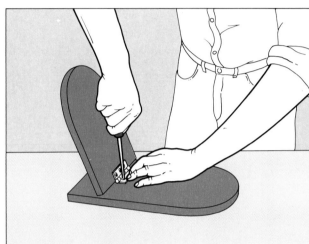

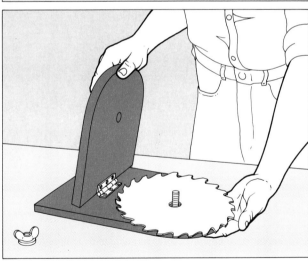

3 Drilling a hole. Close the two boards of the jig. Position the circular-saw blade that is to be sharpened on the jig so that its teeth and gullets extend just beyond the semicircular ends. Mark the position of the central hole of the blade on the jig *(above)* and use an auger bit to drill a hole of the same diameter—usually 12 to 16 mm— through both boards of the jig.

If you need to sharpen other circular-saw blades of different sizes, drill other central holes through the jig to suit each blade.

4 Securing the blade. Put a bolt through one side of the jig, place the circular-saw blade over the bolt, close the jig and secure it with a wing nut. As a guide for sharpening the blade, mark a pencil line on the top edge of the jig at the centre of the semicircular ends.

Before using, secure the protruding square end of the jig in a vice. To remove the blade from the jig or to turn it round while you are sharpening it, unscrew the wing nut and open the jig— there is no need to release the jig from the vice.

2 Making a Multitude of Holes

The average house is riddled with holes. Hundreds of holes are cut through studs, joists and floors as passageways for pipes and cables; larger holes accept the ducts of a modern heating system; innumerable pilot holes accommodate the screws that fasten every manner of object to wooden surfaces; and wide, shallow holes accept metal hardware.

The tools that carpenters use to make holes today are remarkably like those employed for the last several thousand years. Still essential is the auger bit *(opposite)*, invented by the Romans, held in a brace with the adjustable chuck that was perfected more than a century ago by the British. For shallow holes, the tool most often chosen is the chisel, which traces its ancestry back to the Stone Age. Even newly designed bits and cutters resemble their ancient predecessors and are based on the same fundamental principles.

What has changed, and changed radically, is the power that drives the bits and cutters: it is now less often muscle power than electricity. Although many hand tools continue to be popular—and, for some jobs, are necessary—most holes that are drilled today are made with the aid of an electric motor.

The electric drill—heavy, powerful and so fast that many models spin their bits at more than 20 revolutions per second—has taken the tedium out of most drilling and reduced the physical requirements for the job. Unfortunately, it has done so at the expense of accuracy and control. A fixed pillar drill *(page 56)* is a precise tool, but for the portable drills generally used in house carpentry, only vertical drill stands *(page 57)* and drilling jigs can guide a bit to a predetermined depth or hold it firmly in position on a board. Some specialized jigs, such as the ones used by locksmiths to make holes in doors, cost hundreds of pounds; most, such as the ones shown on pages 55–56, are inexpensive and designed for use by home craftsmen; many jigs are home-made. And improvements in the drill itself—a lighter casing, a variable-speed motor and newly designed handles and switches—have restored some of the control lost with the advent of electric motors.

Not all holes are made with drill bits, because not all holes are round. Straight-sided holes are best made by blades rather than bits. Here too, electric power applied to traditional cutters is bringing ease and speed to what had been an arduous job. The large rectangular holes for access to pipework in floors are usually best cut with a power tool—a jigsaw or a portable circular saw *(page 59)*. And even the shallow rectangular holes, called mortises, that hold door hinges and lock plates, can be cut not only in the old way, with a mallet and chisel, but also with one of the newest power tools of all—the router *(page 62)*.

How to Bore Holes Straight, Clean and True

In principle, drilling holes is the simplest operation in carpentry; in practice, it can be one of the most frustrating. No matter how careful your planning and how steady your hand, drilling jobs never quite match textbook rules: the drill will not fit into the cramped space between joists, it veers sideways in a bolt hole that must be perfectly straight, or it whips round and splinters wood as it breaks through a board.

You may be able to avoid these problems if you use the right tools and a repertoire of time-tested carpenter's tricks. Filing flat spots on the round shank of a bit will help it stay put in a power-drill chuck, for example, and a home-made guide like the one on page 56 helps prevent skittering when you drill at a shallow angle.

The basic tool for virtually any drilling task—from making a tiny pilot hole for a wood screw to boring a 60 mm opening for a plumbing pipe—is the portable electric drill. The most common type is a two-speed, 9 mm model with a reversing switch; a variable-speed model affords more control at low speeds.

The portable drill should be equipped with a double-insulating plastic case, which will prevent electric shock if the bit runs into live wires, and a lock on the reversing switch, which will prevent you from changing directions while the motor is running. A well-designed drill has its handle at the back of the case and an auxiliary handle to help you counter the twisting torque from a large bit.

On small jobs, particularly in hard-to-reach places, you may want to drill holes with hand tools. For pilot holes less than 4 mm wide, a particular favourite with carpenters is the push drill—a spring-loaded rod about 300 mm long, with a set of bits stored in its handle. An old-fashioned handwheel brace drill can make holes up to 6 mm wide; it is easier to control than a power drill, but takes more time and effort. For larger holes in cramped quarters, such as the spaces between studs or joists, a swingbrace and an auger bit can be handy if the brace has a ratchet mechanism that allows it to turn in tight quarters.

Although a pillar drill—a large power drill permanently mounted on a fixed stand—is seldom found on commercial construction jobs, it is a workshop tool that can be very helpful in home carpentry. Work must be brought to it, and it cannot handle large panels. However, it is faster, more precise and more versatile than other drills, and, with the aid of stops and jigs, perfect for repetitious tasks such as drilling a set of holes for dowels or louvres. A portable electric drill mounted in a vertical drill stand can perform the same tasks as a pillar drill, but without the same high degree of accuracy and stability.

Almost all of these drills have a three-jawed chuck, which will accept a bit with a cylindrical or hexagonal shank. Some cheaper swingbraces have a pair of jaws, each with a V-shaped notch in the centre; they are designed for the four-sided shank of many auger bits (opposite corners of the bit fit into the notched jaws), but they will also accept a hexagonal shank.

The biggest problem that arises in the course of a drilling job is controlling the bit after it enters the wood. To set the bit for a precise hole, you may need an inexpensive drill guide or a self-centring jig (*page 55*); to control the depth of the hole, you can wrap tape round the bit at the correct depth or you can use a factory-made metal jig that clamps to the bit. Even with these aids, you will occasionally drill a hole in the wrong place or at the wrong angle. To correct such a mistake, glue a tightly fitting dowel or wooden matchstick into the hole, wait for the glue to set, and then redrill the hole starting from scratch.

Choosing the Right Bit

Bits for holes up to 12 mm. A twist bit (*right*)—often called a twist drill or simply a drill—is generally manufactured as an all-purpose tool that will drill through plastic and metal as well as wood. Less common is a bit made for wood that looks like it but has a sharper tip—82 degrees instead of the standard 118 degrees. A brad-point bit (*right, below*)—available in 1 mm intervals from 6 to 12 mm—is a special bit that is preferred for dowel holes and exposed woodwork because it cuts a very smooth hole. The point at the shaft centre guides the bit while the sharp lips at the outside cut the hole.

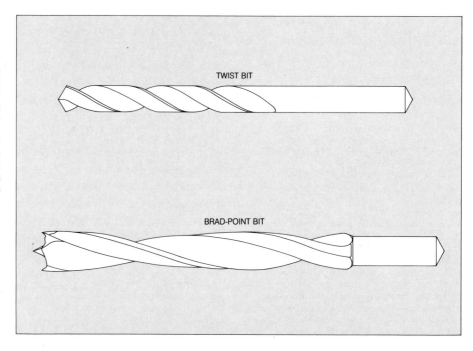

TWIST BIT

BRAD-POINT BIT

Bits for holes up to 25 mm wide. A spade bit, the most versatile and inexpensive of the larger bits, is used with a power drill to cut holes quickly; but it tends to wander in deep holes and to leave ragged edges.

The centre bit is suitable for fast, clean cutting of shallow holes to a depth of about twice the bit diameter, but tends to wander in end-grain. As the bit is pulled into the wood by the screw nose, the single spur scores the hole edges and horizontal cutters scrape away wood chips.

The more expensive single-twist auger bit also has a screw nose, cutters and a single spur; waste is cleared from the hole by the helical twist, whose solid core makes this bit suitable for heavy work and deep holes.

The Jennings Pattern bit works on the same principle as the single-twist auger, but its double twist and two spurs enable it to cut more smoothly and firmly, even in end-grain.

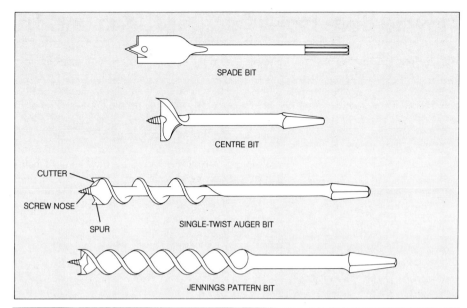

SPADE BIT

CENTRE BIT

CUTTER

SCREW NOSE

SPUR

SINGLE-TWIST AUGER BIT

JENNINGS PATTERN BIT

Two special-purpose bits. A Forstner bit has a flat, disc-shaped head that contains sharp cutting edges. It is expensive and slow, but has certain advantages: it can drill into any sort of grain, including end-grain; it can drill at an angle to the board face without sliding off because its sharpened outer edges dig into the wood; and it makes an almost perfectly flat-bottomed hole—an advantage when you need a large counterbore or are drilling part way through a board.

A saw-tooth centre bit, used mainly in pillar drills, has a sharply pointed tip surrounded by a ring of teeth. It is particularly useful on thin panelling and veneered plywood because it cuts cleanly without shredding the surface.

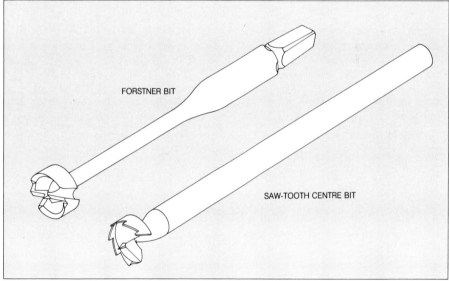

FORSTNER BIT

SAW-TOOTH CENTRE BIT

Countersink bits to recess wood screws. The most common countersink, designed for use with a power drill, is the combination tool *(near right)* that in one step drills a pilot hole, bevels the top of the hole for a screw head and, if required, counterbores a hole for a wooden plug. This tool is essentially a hollow tube, slipped over the shank of a twist bit and fastened with a set-screw; the depth of the pilot hole is determined by the position of the countersink on the shank.

If a pilot hole has already been drilled, or a screw head is too large for a combination countersink or if you need only a few holes, use an ordinary countersink. The traditional type *(centre)* must be used in a hand brace; a newer style *(far right)* is designed for power drills.

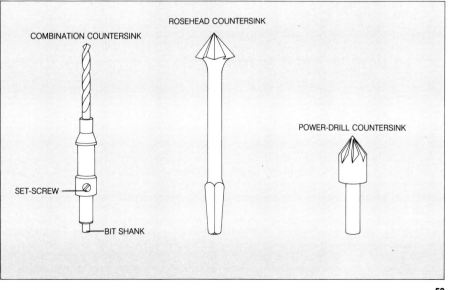

COMBINATION COUNTERSINK

ROSEHEAD COUNTERSINK

POWER-DRILL COUNTERSINK

SET-SCREW

BIT SHANK

Two Ways to Hold a Power Drill

Cradling for a small bit. To start a twist or a brad-point bit, push an awl into the wood at the centre mark for the hole. Grip the drill handle with one hand, cradle the underside of the drill with the other and set the point of the bit in the awl hole. Gently press the drill into the wood at the required angle. If you are using a two-speed drill, set the drill to the fast speed, start the motor and bear down firmly; with a variable-speed drill, gently press the drill into the wood and squeeze the trigger slowly until the bit has made a hole about 3 mm deep, then increase the drill speed to its maximum and bear down firmly. From time to time, clear the waste wood in the hole by pulling back the drill slightly, keeping the motor running, then bearing down again. If drilling right through a board, reduce the pressure but maintain the drill speed as the bit bores through the last few millimetres, to avoid the wood splintering on the other side of the board.

If the hole must be perfectly perpendicular to the wood's surface, have a helper set a combination square against the board and sight the bit against it *(inset)* or one of the jigs opposite.

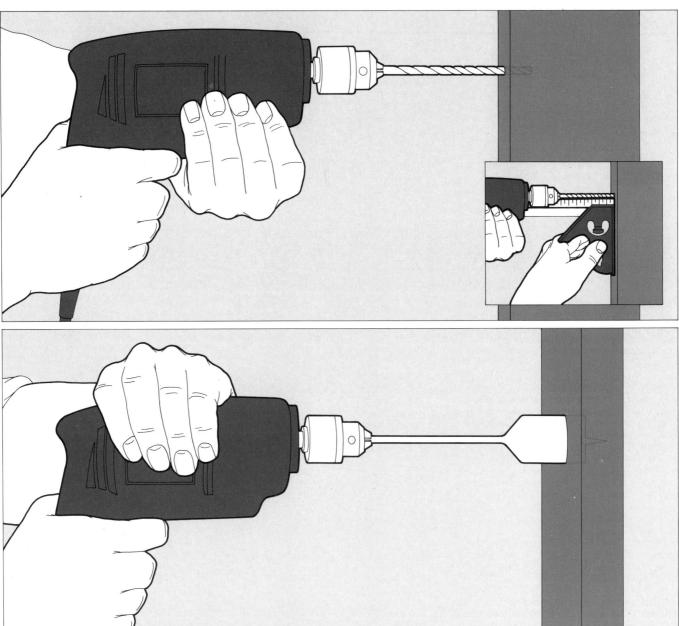

Steadying a large bit. To drive a bit with large cutting edges, such as a spade or Forstner bit, hold the drill handle with one hand and grasp the top of the drill firmly with the other, a grip that resists the twisting tendency of the drill better than the cradling grip illustrated at the top of this page. Position the bit in the awl hole, set the drill at the slow speed and start the motor.

If the bit binds momentarily, pull the drill back a few millimetres and then bear down again. When the bit gets near the other side of the board, reduce the pressure and brace yourself; the drill may jerk and bind as it breaks through. Turn off the drill as soon as the bit is cleanly through the board.

The Use of Hand Drills

Using a handwheel brace drill. For a few small holes, many carpenters prefer this old-fashioned manual drill. Set the bit point in an awl hole, press the drill lightly against the wood and turn the crank clockwise. When the bit breaks through the board, continue to crank clockwise as you pull the bit out—cranking anticlockwise will release the bit from the chuck.

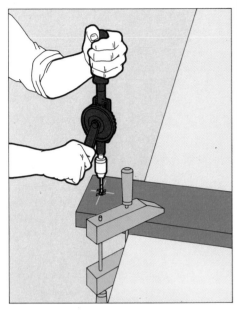

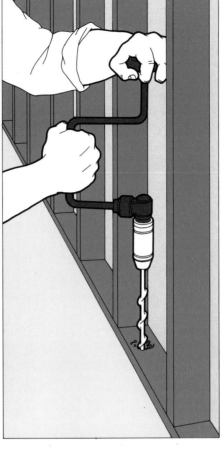

A ratchet swingbrace. For cramped quarters, where there is too little space to align a power drill properly, use a brace, adjusting the ratchet setting of the brace for a clockwise sweep. Set the feed screw of the auger bit into the awl hole, press hard on the brace head with one hand and slowly swing the handle in half circles with the other until the feed screw is buried in the wood and the bit begins to bore. If the feed screw does not dig into the wood, make sure you are holding the brace steady; side-to-side movement loosens the screw. When the bit breaks through the board, reverse the ratchet adjustment and pull the handle to back the bit out.

Guides and Jigs for Precision Work

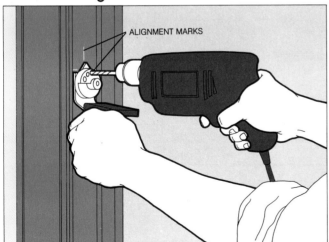

ALIGNMENT MARKS

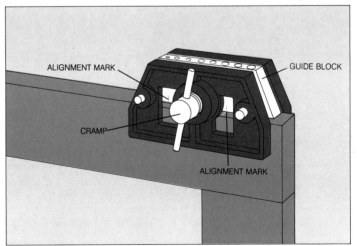

ALIGNMENT MARK

GUIDE BLOCK

CRAMP

ALIGNMENT MARK

A hand-held drill guide. A revolving selector in this guide has holes of the common sizes of small bits to position a bit for perfect right-angle drilling. Marks on the guide can be aligned with marks on the wood to help locate the hole.

You can easily make a hand-held guide for frequently used bits by drilling holes of the required sizes in a 200 by 25 by 25 mm wood offcut; use a combination square *(opposite page, above)* to ensure that the holes are exactly perpendicular.

A self-centring dowelling jig. The guide block of this jig has holes for several common dowel sizes and is automatically centred by a cramp; it sets dowel holes perfectly centred in board edges—as for corner joints on a door. To align the jig, mark a square line across the board edge for each hole, line up the matching guide-block mark, and tighten the cramp. Drill the hole with a twist or a brad-point bit.

A home-made angle jig. Cut perfectly square ends on a scrap of 75 by 75 mm timber about 300 mm long and, about 25 mm from one end, drill a hole of the desired diameter at a perfect right angle to the face of the board. Set a sliding bevel to the desired angle of the hole you are planning to drill and hold the handle of the bevel against the end of the board, so that the blade crosses the path of the bored straight hole; draw a line along the blade. Using a mitre box, cut the 75 by 75 mm scrap along the line *(page 28, Step 1)*.

Temporarily nail the jig to the board you plan to drill, with its sawn face down *(inset)*, and use the hole as a guide for the drill bit.

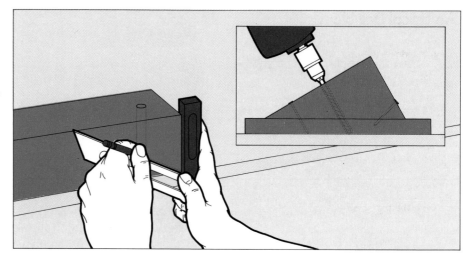

For Perfect Holes, a Pillar Drill

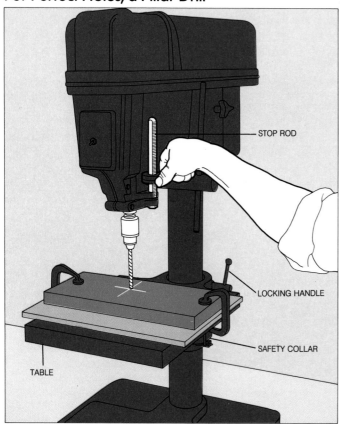

STOP ROD

LOCKING HANDLE

SAFETY COLLAR

TABLE

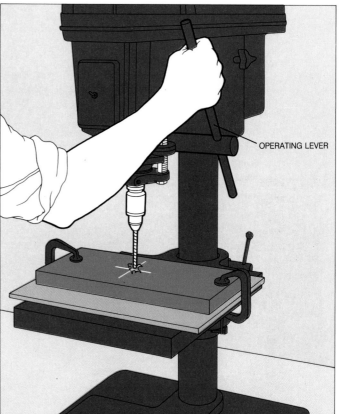

OPERATING LEVER

1 Adjusting the table. With the bit in the drill chuck, fasten the board to the pillar drill table with G-cramps. Hold the table and loosen the locking handle that fastens the table to the column, then raise or lower the table by simultaneously lifting it and swinging it from side to side. When the tip of the drill bit is about 6 mm above the board, tighten the locking handle and move the safety collar on the column to a position just beneath the table. Adjust the stop nut and the lock nut on the calibrated stop rod to set the depth of the planned hole.

2 Drilling the hole. With the drill off, loosen the cramps that hold the board and turn the operating lever until the bit almost touches the wood; then shift the board to clamp it with the centre of the planned hole directly beneath the tip of the bit. Let the bit rise to the stop, turn the motor on and slowly lower the bit into the wood, using light pressure on the operating lever.

A Vertical Drill Stand

Fixing a portable drill. Fasten the stand base to the worktable with bolts or screws. Secure the wood on the base with cramps or, as here, a special vice that can be bolted to the stand base. Fix the drill in the collar cramp and tighten the bolts, then move the mounting bracket down the support shaft until the drill bit is about 6 mm above the board. Set the gauge for the depth of the planned hole by locking the depth stop on the support shaft or by setting the calibrated dial on the operating lever to correspond to a mark on the shaft—as the drill is lowered, the dial will indicate the depth of the hole. Switch on the drill and lower the operating lever to drill the hole.

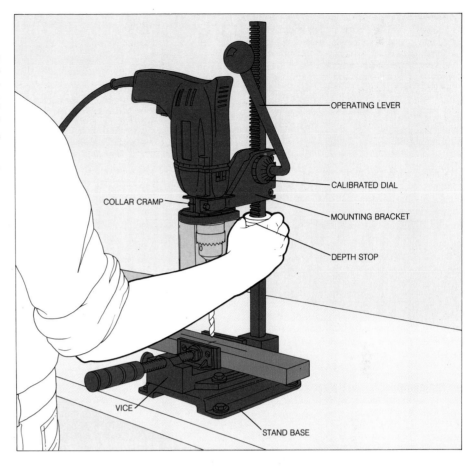

Set-ups for Angled Holes

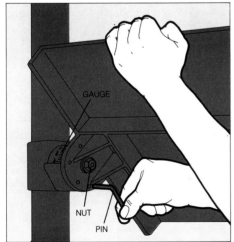

A factory-made tilting table. If your pillar drill or vertical stand has a table that pivots on the cramp that fastens it to the column, as in the model shown here, loosen the nut at the base of the table; remove the index pin from its hole in the base and tilt the table to the desired angle. Slide the index pin through the hole for the angle and tighten the nut; if there is no hole for the index pin, set the pin aside, align the arrow on the tabletop with the correct reading on the angle gauge and tighten the nut.

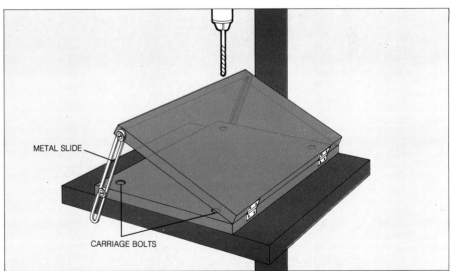

A home-made tilting table. To make a tilting table, cut two pieces of wood, 225 by 25 by 300 mm long; hinge them together lengthwise. Set the assembly on the pillar drill table with the hinges at one side; on the lower board, mark the location of the table's mounting holes. Drill and counterbore a hole at each mark so that the board can be fastened to the table with 6 mm carriage bolts and wing nuts.

Fasten 200 mm metal desk-lid slides to the opposite sides of the boards with wood screws and washers. To use the table, temporarily bolt the lower board to the drill table, raise the upper board to the angle you want, checking with a sliding bevel, then lock the upper board by tightening the wood screws of the slides. Fasten the work to the angled table with G-cramps and drill it in the usual way.

Four Ways to Make Large Holes

Although the spade and auger bits shown on pages 52 to 55 can bore holes as wide as 35 mm, most holes more than 25 mm wide are made with a different set of tools. For holes between 25 and 75 mm in diameter, needed mainly for plumbing drains and vents, special bits are used; openings that are still larger than that—circular for flues and round ducts, rectangular for service access in flooring and panelling—are cut with saws.

The drilled holes ordinarily require an electric drill—either the standard 9 mm size or, for particularly wide, deep holes, a slower, heavy-duty 12 mm drill, available at hire shops. The preferred bits are hole saws—hollow metal cylinders with saw-like teeth, which fit on to a separate shaft called a mandrel *(right)*. Hole saws can be fitted with such accessories as bit extensions—some as long as 1 metre—for very deep or inaccessible holes. If you must drill an odd-sized hole or lack the right hole saw for a standard one, you can substitute a brace and an expansive bit *(below, right)*

which has a cutter that is adjustable to a range of diameters.

For sawing holes, the compass saw on page 34 will serve, but a faster, more common tool is a jigsaw, used either freehand or with a yoke-like guide that guarantees perfect circles. A jigsaw can also be used for large rectangular holes, but professional carpenters prefer a portable circular saw; to start each side of the cut, they start the motor and slowly lower the blade of the saw into the middle of a panel, making what is called a pocket cut, then finish the side of the opening by using the saw in the normal way.

Bits for Holes up to 75 mm Wide

A hole saw. Slide the mandrel through the centre of the hole saw *(inset)* and secure it with the mandrel nut (on some large saws, the mandrel screws into the hole saw), then clamp the shank of the mandrel in the chuck of the drill. Mark the centre of the hole with an awl and start the hole with the twist bit at the end of the mandrel; when the saw begins to cut, grasp the drill firmly to resist its twist. When the twist bit breaks through the wood, withdraw the saw and finish the job from the other side.

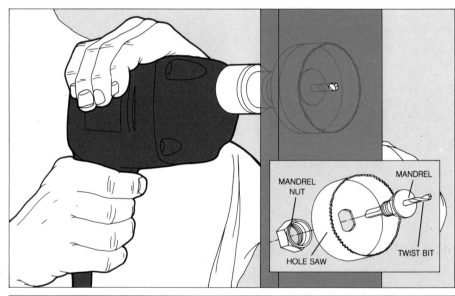

MANDREL NUT
MANDREL
HOLE SAW
TWIST BIT

An expansive bit. Loosen the set-screw at the head of the bit *(inset)* and slide the cutter along its groove to the diameter of the desired hole, as indicated on the cutter gauge, then tighten the set-screw; if precision is essential to the job, check the cutter setting by drilling a trial hole.

Use the bit as you would an auger bit *(page 55, top right)* but take special pains to keep the brace perfectly vertical, so that the cutter shaves away the wood evenly. As the hole deepens, bear down hard on the brace; otherwise the feed screw will strip out of the wood and stop pulling.

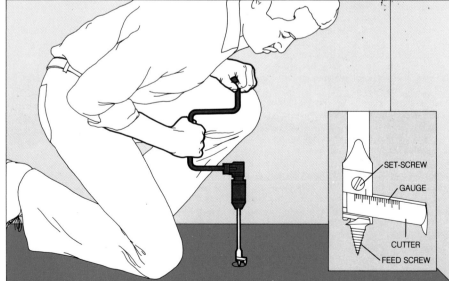

SET-SCREW
GAUGE
CUTTER
FEED SCREW

Saws for Openings any Size You Need

A jigsaw guide for a perfect circle. One end of the guide on the right is fastened to the centre of a planned hole, and the other is fastened to a jigsaw. To set up the guide, drill a 6 mm hole at a point on the edge of the planned hole and insert the jigsaw blade in this starter hole. Slide the guide through the slots in the saw base plate, drive a nail through one of the holes at the end of the guide into the exact centre of the planned hole and clamp the guide to the saw base plate. Start the saw and cut the hole by pivoting the guide round the nail.

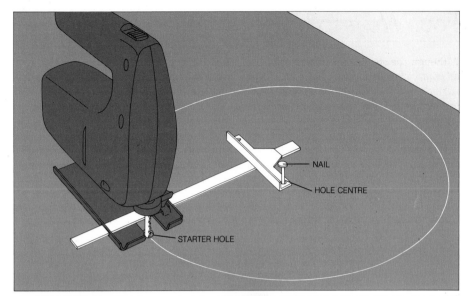

NAIL

HOLE CENTRE

STARTER HOLE

A rectangular hole with a jigsaw. For a hole whose sides are less than 200 mm, mark the outline of the hole with a pencil and combination square and drill a 6 mm hole at each corner. Insert the saw blade in one hole and cut along the outline; at each corner, turn the saw off and turn it to cut the adjacent side of the rectangle.

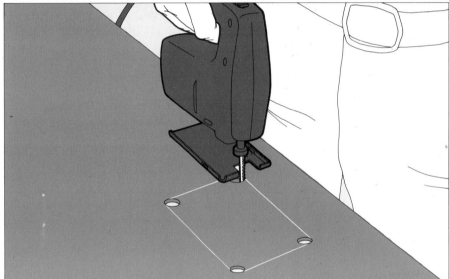

A rectangular hole with a circular saw. To cut a hole with sides longer than 200 mm, set the blade of the saw 6 mm deeper than the thickness of the wood. Rest the toe of the saw on the wood, holding the heel and blade above the wood. Retract the blade guard with your free hand and align the blade directly above one side of the proposed hole. Start the saw, slowly lower the blade into the wood until the base plate rests flat on the wood and cut to the corner of the hole.

Caution: this is the most dangerous part of the job; hold the saw with special firmness and be prepared to turn it off immediately if it goes out of control. Remove the saw and cut the other sides in the same way. Where precision is important, stop short of the corners and finish the cuts with a compass saw or jigsaw.

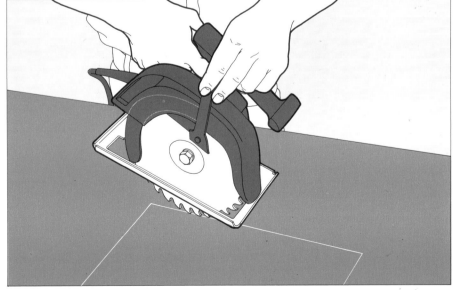

The Rectangular Holes Called Mortises

There are several kinds of the rectangular holes called mortises, and the kind you have to make determines the tools and techniques you should use. Some mortises are precise but shallow, like, for instance, the recess that houses a hinge. Others are rough and deep, like the pocket for the end of a hand-hewn beam. Still others are both precise and deep, like the mortises in door and window joints.

The most common tool for both deep and shallow mortises is a chisel. However, shallow mortises can be cut quickly and accurately by a router *(page 62)*—the router gives round corners, but you can buy round-cornered hinges and other hardware to fit router-cut mortises. Deep mortises are made with a drill and chisel *(page 63)*, a mallet and special mortise chisel *(page 119)*, or a mortiser—a pillar drill attachment that performs the seemingly impossible feat of drilling a square hole *(page 65)*.

The best all-round chisel is a firmer. It has a sturdy, flat-faced blade that can be sharpened again and again *(pages 90–93)* and is virtually indestructible in normal use. For intricate work, such as angled housings, use a bevel-edged chisel, which is bevelled along the sides as well as on the cutting edge. Both firmer and bevel-edged chisels come with either wooden or plastic handles. A large, rectangular wooden mallet must be used on wooden handles, and although plastic handles can be safely hit with a hammer, it is better to use a mallet on bevel-edged chisels—it is less likely to drive the chisel too deep.

For deep precision mortising, as in the joints of window sashes or panelled doors *(page 118)*, the quickest and simplest tool is the special mortise chisel, which must be used with a wooden mallet. Together they cut and prise out wood in a single step, usually for a mortise exactly as wide as the chisel blade. The same shape as a firmer, but longer and heavier, the mortise chisel can take hard mallet blows without twisting as it enters the wood, and the mortise it makes is so smooth that it very rarely needs paring.

More expensive but most precise of all for accurate deep mortises is the mortiser attachment on a pillar drill. Fortunately, one size will do many jobs—depth is adjustable, and it is possible, by boring square adjoining holes, to build mortises of any width or length.

Chiselling a Shallow Mortise

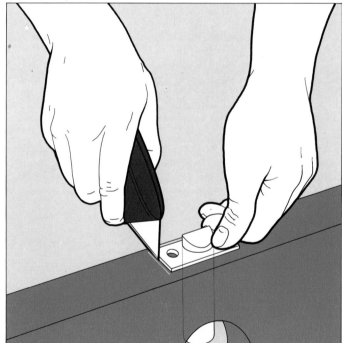

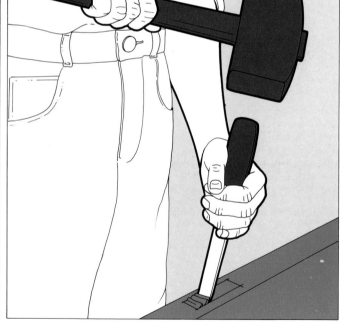

1 **Marking the mortise.** Press the hardware—in this example, the face plate of a door catch—against the wood and score along its edges with a trimming knife, using repeated light strokes to cut the wood fibre so that the chisel will be less likely to splinter the surface.

If the mortise will be open on one side, as for a door hinge, mark the mortise depth on the open side with a marking gauge *(page 20)*.

2 **Scoring.** Set the blade of a firmer chisel vertically across the mortise outline about 6 mm in from one end, with the bevel facing inwards. Angle the chisel towards the bevel side and away from your striking hand. Tap the chisel to a depth slightly less than the thickness of the hardware. Working towards the opposite end of the outline, repeat this cut at 10 mm intervals to within 10 mm of the end.

3 Removing the chips. Reverse the chisel. Starting at the far end of the mortise and holding the chisel so that the bevel is almost horizontal and is at the full depth of the mortise, remove the chips made by the cuts in Step 2.

4 Squaring the cut. Set a bevel-edged chisel at one end of the mortise outline with the bevel facing into the cleared area. Keeping the blade upright, tap the chisel with the mallet to square off and clear the end of the mortise. Repeat for the opposite end of the mortise.

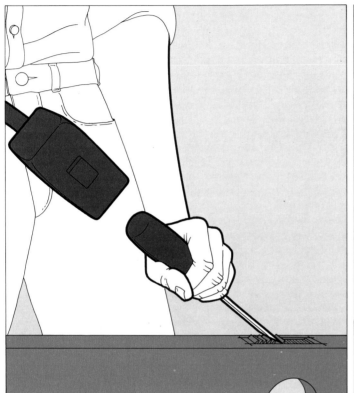

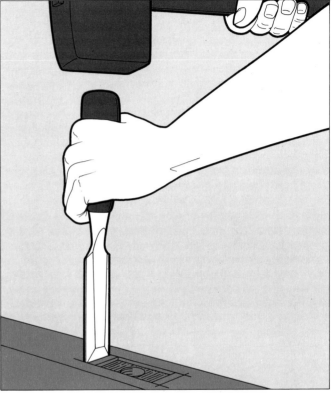

Finishing the Mortise

Paring a closed mortise. Hold the bevel-edged chisel, bevel down, with the heel of one hand against the end of the handle and the thumb of the other on the flat side of the blade. Make light shaving strokes parallel to the grain along the bottom of the mortise so that you produce a smooth, even surface. Test-fit the hardware occasionally to check the depth of the mortise.

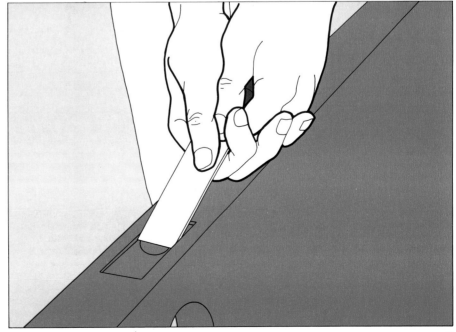

Paring an open mortise. Position the chisel, bevel up, at the open side of the mortise, setting the flat side of the blade even with the mortise bottom. Grip the chisel as you would for a closed mortise, holding the index finger of your forward hand as far back from the cutting edge as the width of the mortise, so that on each stroke you can stop the blade when the edge reaches the far side. Make light shaving strokes, working at about an 80 degree angle to the grain.

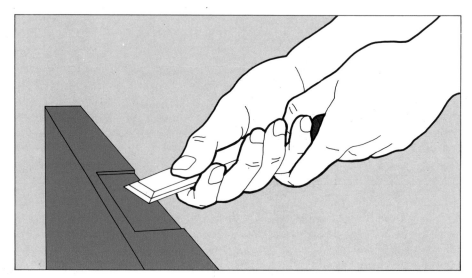

Routing a Shallow Mortise

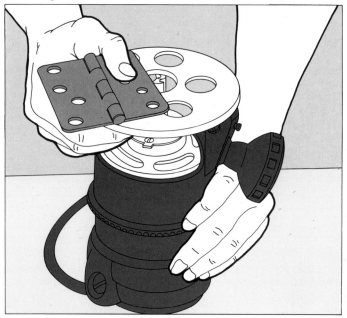

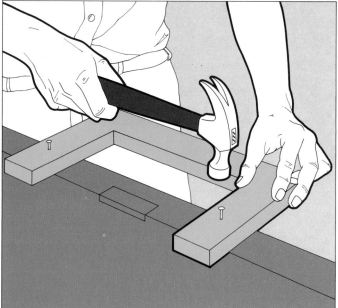

1 Setting the bit. Fit a straight bit in a router, hold the router with its bottom up, and set the hardware—in this case, a hinge—alongside the bit as a guide for adjusting the cutting depth.

Score the outline of the mortise *(page 60, Step 1)*. If you intend to leave the mortise corners round for round-cornered hardware, use especially light strokes at the corners—if the knife point is pressed too hard, it will tend to follow a straight path between fibres and stray from the rounded outlines.

2 Making a guide. From a 400 by 200 mm piece of blockboard or plywood, cut out a section which is equal to the length of the hinge plus the router base-plate diameter, and the width of the hinge plus the base-plate diameter.

Carefully centre the cut-away area of the guide over the mortise outline, and fasten the guide temporarily to the timber edge with two 25 mm wire nails.

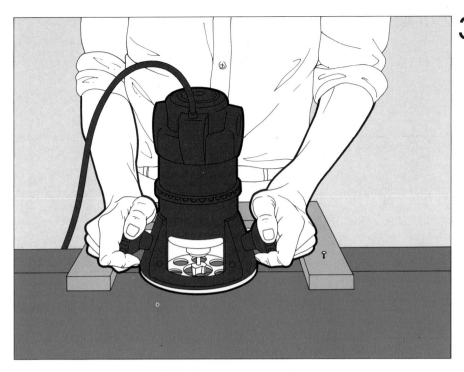

3 **Routing out the wood.** For a closed mortise, set the router bit over the board at the centre of the mortise outline, with the router slightly tilted; turn on the motor and lower the bit into the wood. For an open mortise, start the cut at the edge of the board, as on page 85, top. With the base plate flat on the wood, move the router along the edges of the guide to remove the wood within the outlined area. As you work, try as far as possible to keep the outline marks between the bit and your line of vision, but do not lean completely over the router.

If you need to have square corners in your mortise, use a chisel to square off the rounded corners that are left by the router.

A Mortise in Rough Timber

1 **Starting with a drill.** Choose a drill bit as close in size to the mortise width as you can, mark the bit shank with tape for the mortise depth, and drill repeatedly inside the mortise outline. Locate the holes to barely touch one another and to come within 1 mm of the outline of the mortise.

2 **Finishing with a chisel.** Remove most of the remaining wood with a firmer chisel and a wooden mallet, holding the chisel vertical with the bevel facing into the mortise. Then, hold the chisel in two hands and pare the sides of the mortise roughly vertical.

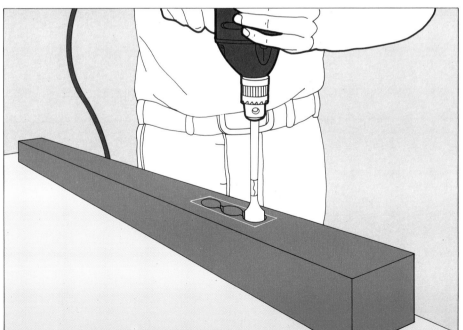

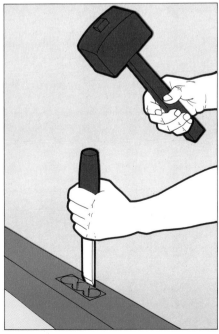

Cutting Deep Holes with a Mortise Chisel

1 **Marking the mortise.** To fit the mortise precisely to the width of the chisel blade, mark it with precision tools: outline the sides with a mortising gauge *(page 119)*, and the ends with a combination square and a trimming knife; then use the knife and square to score a series of lines across the outline. Score the first line across the centre of the outline; then, working towards the ends of the mortise, score lines at 3 mm intervals, with the last lines about 6 mm from the ends.

Use tape to mark the depth of the mortise on the back and front of the mortise-chisel blade.

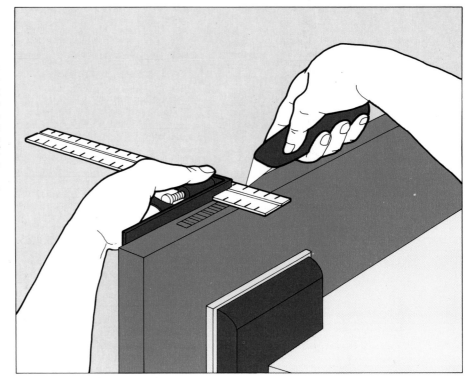

2 **Aligning the chisel.** Use a chisel that is exactly as wide as the mortise. Standing at one end of the mortise outline, hold the handle with one hand and use the other to set the blade, bevel facing away, in the centre score line.

Check to be sure that the sides of the chisel align with the sides of the outline.

3 **Cutting.** Hold the chisel blade exactly vertical and strike the end of the handle hard, using a wooden mallet with a large rectangular head. For the next cut, angle the chisel blade slightly away from you on the next score line on the far side, then drive the chisel into the wood to make a V-shaped notch in the centre of the mortise outline. This starting notch will receive waste wood from the following cuts *(inset)*.

With the bevel still facing away from you, continue driving the chisel into the score lines up to the last line, 6 mm from the far end. Then turn the chisel round so that the bevel faces towards you; chisel out the chips back to the centre, and continue driving the chisel into the score lines to within 6 mm of the near end. Reverse the chisel again and work back to the centre, chiselling out the remaining chips.

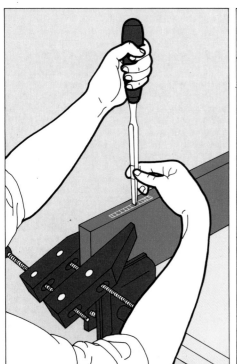

4 Squaring and cleaning the mortise. With the bevel facing towards the centre, hold the chisel upright at one end of the mortise outline; then drive in the chisel with the mallet to make a vertical cut. Square off the opposite end in the same way.

To protect the mortise edge while cleaning out the ends, place a scrap of timber just outside the mortise outline. Holding the scrap in one hand and the chisel in the other, place the chisel bevel down in the cleared area and lever out any remaining chips *(right)*.

To make a mortise deeper than 15 mm, chisel out to a uniform depth of 15 mm, square and clear the ends, then repeat the procedure until you reach the required depth.

Drilling Square Holes with a Pillar Drill Mortiser

A mortising attachment. In the assembly on the right, a yoke clamped to the neck of a pillar drill holds a square, hollow chisel below the chuck of the drill. The chuck itself holds a specialized drill bit that turns within the chisel. While the tip of the bit cuts a round hole, the chisel chops corners on each side, and the auger-like shaft of the bit forces wood chips up and out through a slot in the front of the chisel. The depth adjustment of the pillar drill sets the depth of the mortise; long or wide mortises are made by drilling square holes side by side.

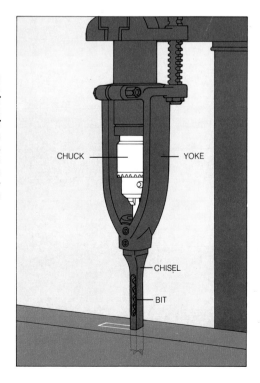

Professional Methods for Sharpening Drill Bits

Drilling with a blunt bit takes unnecessary time and effort; worse, it can break the bit, cause the drill to slip or ruin a drill motor. Small, inexpensive bits should be discarded and replaced when blunt; larger, more costly bits should be sharpened. And though a professional sharpener can do the job for you, you can easily learn to do a professional job yourself.

Part of the job consists in knowing exactly how the bit was shaped to begin with—the lengths and angles of the cutting edges on the tip of the bit. These anatomical details are just as important as the sharpness of the bit: for example, a bit with unequal cutting edges will work off-centre and cut an oversized hole; a bit with inadequate clearance between its head and shaft will bind and overheat.

Bits which have delicate edges and complex shapes must be sharpened by hand, preferably using files and oilstones which are especially fitted to the particular bit. An auger-bit file and an oilstone, for example, will hone the cutting edges of an auger bit without causing any damage to the adjacent parts. (And since most brand-new auger bits should get a preliminary sharpening before their first use, these tools are a worthwhile investment.) Triangular stones and files are ideal for sharp-

ening the fluted edges of a countersink bit.

To restore the cutting edges of twist and spade bits—the ones usually used with an electric drill—you will need a grinding wheel with a tool rest and a few simple accessories. A home-made jig (opposite page, bottom) sets the correct angles for a twist bit, and a drill gauge—essentially a combination of a protractor and a ruler—checks the angles and lip lengths of the sharpened bit; a stop collar that sets a bit firmly against the tool rest (page 69, above) will enable you to grind the wings of a spade bit symmetrically.

Caution: the innocent-looking grinding wheel is a dangerous tool because its high-speed rotation—generally more than 3,500 revolutions per minute (rpm)—generates powerful centrifugal force. It can strike off fast-moving, hot bits of metal and, if damaged, it can disintegrate, exploding like a grenade in a shower of lethal fragments. When using one, follow all safety precautions (opposite page, right).

If you are buying a new wheel, choose a 125 to 175 mm aluminium oxide wheel with a grit rating of 100 and a vitrified, or glasslike bond (the bond is the medium used to form the grains of abrasive material into a stable wheel). Before mounting the wheel, check it visually for cracks or

chips, then suspend it on a dowel or pencil inserted through the centre hole and tap it lightly with a wooden mallet or screwdriver handle. Unless it is a wheel bonded with rubber or organic material, you should hear a clear metallic ring. If it is chipped or cracked or fails to ring clearly, you must replace it.

After mounting and using the wheel, check it periodically for roundness and wear. A shiny, glazed look indicates that the pores of the wheel are clogged with metal dust and particles. A glazed wheel will overheat and ruin a bit applied to it; you can recondition the wheel with a tool called a starwheel dresser, which hooks on to the tool rest and scrapes the wheel face with sharp, star-shaped steel teeth. Do not dress a wheel down more than 25 mm below its original diameter.

Between sharpenings, store your bits in partitioned boxes or in canvas rolls, and clean them regularly to retard the dulling process. Use fine glass paper or an emery cloth to remove rust and wood sap. To clean the twist of a bit, dip an old cloth in paraffin then in powdered pumice (available at ironmongers or chemists), and wrap it round the flutes; to clean the screw point of an auger bit, use a piece of stiff paper or an old toothbrush.

Cutting Angles of Basic Bits

A twist bit. Two rounded ridges called "lands" or "margins" spiral around the central shaft, or web, of a twist bit. At the cutting end, the lands are ground to meet at an angle of 118 degrees (82 degrees on some special wood bits), forming two flats, called point surfaces, that converge along a centre chisel edge. The front edge of each point surface, called the cutting lip, is slightly higher than the back edge, or heel. The clearance between the two allows the body of the bit to follow easily behind the lips as they cut away wood; the shavings move along the spirals of the lands and out of the hole.

The cutting lips are naturally the first parts of the bit to become blunt—the edges of the lips become slightly rounded, their clearance above the heels decreases and the bit binds and overheats.

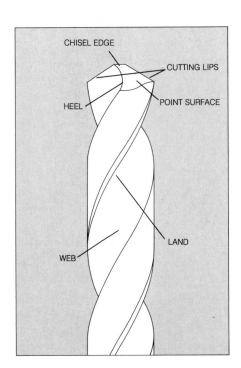

A spade bit. This flat-bladed bit has a point, or spur, that bites into the wood and steadies the bit on centre while wing-like cutting lips chisel the hole. The edges of the lips and the spur are bevelled at an angle of 8 degrees; on most spade bits, the cutting lips are perpendicular to the axis of the bit, but in some they are set at an angle. On a blunt spade bit the bevels are slightly rounded and the lips slightly unequal and out of line.

An auger bit. A central screw point draws the auger bit into the wood; at the edge of the hole, spurs score the wood ahead of the cutting lips, which cut wood within the scored circle. The twisted throat carries chips out of the hole.

The bit should be sharpened when the edges of the spurs and cutting lips are blunt or chipped. The spurs should project far enough to score the wood fibres thoroughly before the cutting lips make contact; the lips should be equal in length and bevelled at the same angle.

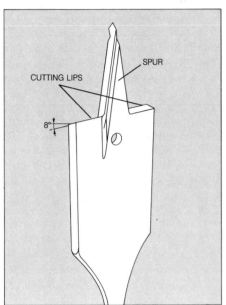

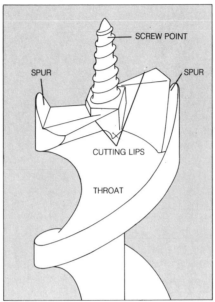

Grinding a Twist Bit

1 Setting up a guide block. Use a sliding bevel and a pencil to draw a line across the tool rest of the grinding wheel at an angle to the face of the wheel that is half of the correct angle for the bit tip—for most twist bits, set the sliding bevel to 59 degrees; for special wood bits, to 41 degrees. To the left of this line, at 6 mm intervals, lay out several parallel lines at an angle 12 degrees less than the first—usually this will be a 47 degree angle. Use a G-cramp to secure a small block of wood to the tool rest, at the right of and flush with the 59 degree line.

For twist bits that are smaller than 3 mm, omit the parallel lines but adjust the tool rest so that the back edge is 12 degrees lower than the front edge.

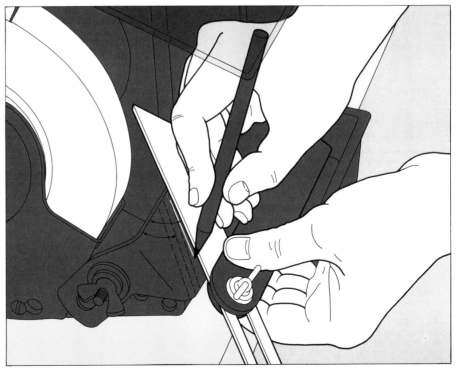

2 **Grinding the bit.** Wearing safety goggles or a face mask, start the motor and let the grinding wheel run until it reaches a steady speed. Hold the shank of the twist bit in your right hand and use your left to position the bit against the guide block with one cutting lip perfectly horizontal. Slowly move the bit forwards until it makes contact with the wheel, then simultaneously rotate the shank of the bit clockwise and swing the entire bit parallel to the 47 degree lines. Time the movements so that when the bit reaches the 47 degree position you have rolled from the cutting lip to the heel of a point surface *(inset)*.

Position the bit with the other cutting lip horizontal and grind the second point surface in the same way. Alternate the passes between the point surfaces, grinding each equally until the bit is sharp. After each two or three passes, stop to cool the bit.

Position a bit smaller than 3 mm in the same way, but do not swing or rotate the bit.

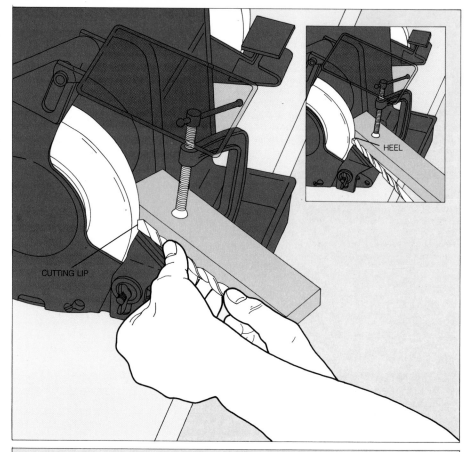

3 **Checking the bit.** Set the bit in the lip corner of a drill gauge to compare the lengths of the cutting lips, then turn the bit slightly to check the clearance at the heels *(inset)*. If the lips or clearances are unequal, regrind the bit.

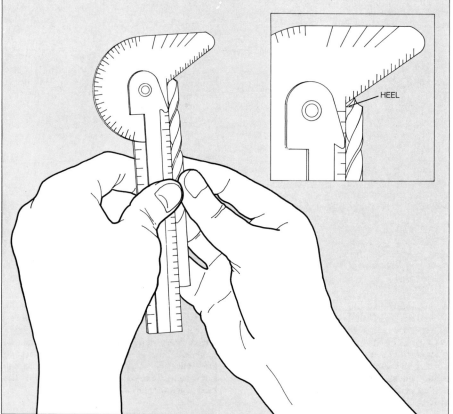

Correcting the Bevel of a Spade Bit

Grinding the edge bevels. Set the tool rest at an angle of 8 degrees to the horizontal, with the higher end facing the grinding wheel, and tighten a stop collar on the shank of a spade bit so that when the stop bears against the edge of the rest, the bit's cutting lips will bear against the wheel face. Hold the bit flat on the tool rest and apply a cutting lip, bevel facing down, to the wheel face. When one lip has been ground, turn the bit over to grind the other lip. To grind the bevels at the edges of the spur, swing the bit about 90 degrees and guide it against the wheel freehand *(inset)*. Turn the bit over to grind the opposite spur edge, taking care to grind both edges equally so that the spur remains centred.

Remove burrs on the spurs and lips with one or two light strokes of an oilstone on the flat faces.

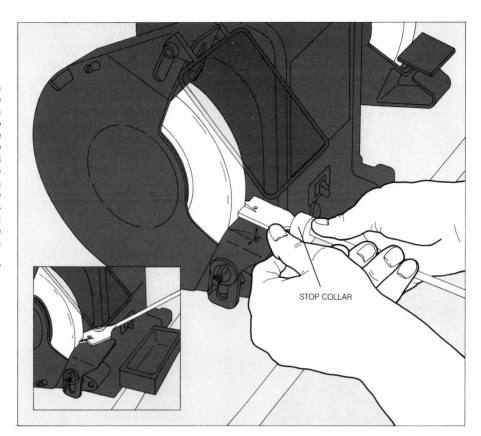

STOP COLLAR

Filing Auger Bits and Countersinks

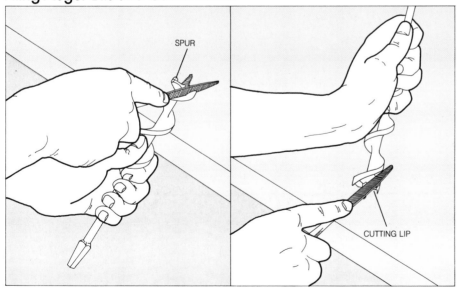

SPUR

CUTTING LIP

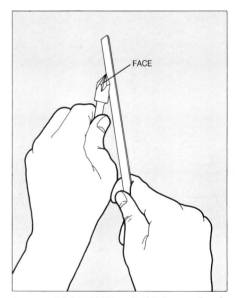

FACE

An auger bit. Hold the throat of the bit against the edge of a worktable so that the cutting head projects above the table, and make straight, even, pushing strokes with an auger-bit file to sharpen the inside edge of each spur *(above)*. Do not file the outsides of the spurs, as this will reduce the size of the hole that the head bores and cause the shaft of the bit to bind.

Rest the head of the auger bit on the work-table and file the top of the cutting lips to a sharp edge bevelled at about 45 degrees *(above)*. Take special care to file bevels that are equal in length and angle, and make sure you do not undercut the base of the screw point. Do not file the underside of the cutting lips next to the screw point. To complete the job, lightly whet the filed edges with an auger-bit oilstone.

A countersink bit. Holding the bit in your hand, use a small triangular oilstone to sharpen the faces of the fluted cutting edges with light, even strokes; take special care to keep the stone flat against each face. Do not sharpen the backs of the cutting edges, as this may alter their height so that they will not cut, but complete the job by removing the burr from each back with a single, light stroke of the stone.

3

The Knack of Shaping Wood

Planes that smooth curves. Spokeshaves, miniature variations of the everyday plane, are made with soles, or base plates, so short that they can follow tight curves—here, the curved edges of decorative shelf brackets. The top spokeshave has a flat sole, for convex curves and for some narrow straight cuts such as the chamfer demonstrated on page 79; the spokeshave in front of it has a slightly rounded sole, for concave surfaces.

Wood has always been special—spirits were said to live in it, and gods and demigods were said to protect the trees that produced it. In part, this special reverence stems from the many uses of wood, from buildings to bowls, but certainly another reason must be the elegance and simplicity with which wood achieves these practical ends. It can be shaped into graceful forms. Its edges can be smoothed to meet for a seemingly seamless corner, or they can be shaped to lock in a grip that will endure over the centuries.

Of the hundreds of such jointing techniques that were once essential to the house carpenter's work, only a few remain in common use: mitres, which fit moulding round angles; kerfing, which flexes boards for curves; rebates, housings and grooves, three related shapes used for joints; and mortises and tenons, which lock joints in moving assemblies such as windows and doors. All of them are ancient, still known by their old names. And, ironically, most of them are created today either by one of the oldest of tools, the plane, or by one of the newest, the router. The two tools are dissimilar. The plane (as well as its variant, the spokeshave) is a blade in a holder. The router is a spinning bit.

The plane is often the symbol of a woodworker's highest craftsmanship, not only for what it can do but also for its beauty as a tool. As early as the Roman era, the plane was a sophisticated instrument, and in Baroque times it flourished into a wide range of shapes and sizes to carve the mouldings for lavish palaces. By the 18th century, woodworkers made a separate plane for every wood shape, from delicate beading, to structural joints.

The tools themselves were revered. Each workman made his own, fashioning each to fit his grip. With his plane the woodworker used his eye, his ear, but most of all his hands, and when he used it he had what admirers called the knack—the precise art of forming wood to the perfect shape, whether for a rebate joint in a doorjamb or the curves of an intricate architrave round a window.

The whisper of a plane is now often replaced by the whir of a router. Electric motors and toughened steel led the way to speed in fashioning wood. And the router bit cuts so smoothly that it simultaneously shapes and finishes, making sanding almost superfluous.

Yet even in the machine age, using the plane and the router calls for skills. Both tools require adjustments so precise that only the eye can serve as arbiter. With both tools the worker needs to know how hard to press against the wood and how fast to push along the fibres. Tools do not have the knack: craftsmen do. Once achieved, the knack leads to some of the most beautiful results in woodworking: a shape that perfectly fits its function, a look of warmth and rhythm, and a feel that only fingers can sense is truly smooth.

Planing a Board to Lie Flat and Fit Tight

For trimming and smoothing wood, no tool is more accurate than a hand plane with a razor-sharp blade. It is the ideal tool for such jobs as levelling a surface for a shelf; shaving an edge, such as the narrow top of a drawer; or, by using a technique called "shooting" *(page 74)*, shaping the edge of a board exactly perpendicular to its face.

A hand plane's major shortcoming is its reliance on muscle power; on big jobs, such as smoothing the faces of large boards or trimming doors, you may want to speed and ease the work with a portable power plane *(page 77)*.

Ordinary jobs are handled by two types of hand planes—two-hand bench planes and smaller, simpler, one-hand block planes. Bench planes come in a variety of sizes, but all have the same basic design. The blade, called an iron, is mounted about 45 degrees from the horizontal with its bevel side down; it protrudes through a slit called the mouth, in the bottom, or sole. As the plane moves forwards over the wood, the blade prises up a thin shaving that is lifted and curled by a second iron, called the cap iron, which has a rounded "nose" rather than a cutting edge.

The depth of the cutting blade, its distance from the front of the mouth, and its position with respect to the cap-iron nose determine exactly how the wood is cut. The most versatile of the bench planes is the 350 mm jack plane, long and heavy enough for straightening edges and levelling surfaces, yet light enough for smoothing, a job requiring many fine, careful strokes.

The block plane is a one-hand tool originally designed for smoothing butcher's blocks made by piecing together short boards, end-grain up. Still the tool of choice for small end-grain jobs, the block plane is also used for light trimming and for smoothing plywood edges. To crosscut the exposed fibres of an end-grain, the iron is set at a lower angle to the wood than that of a bench plane, and the bevel of the cutting edge faces upwards. A good block plane will have an adjustable blade depth and mouth opening, and also a lateral-adjusting lever *(page 76)*.

Whatever plane you use, the general rules for working remain the same. Cut with the grain wherever possible, to avoid tearing the wood fibre; if the grain changes direction along the length of a board, change the direction of your stroke. Let the feel of the plane skimming the wood be a guide: you should push forwards and yet slightly sideways at the same time. Planing should never be hard work. If you plane against the grain, you will immediately feel a roughness and hardness in the cut. When planing faces or broad edges, jobs in which the entire sole is in contact with the wood, rub beeswax or candlewax on the sole to reduce friction.

When you have finished planing or are interrupted in the course of a job, set the plane on its side to avoid damaging the iron. Test the trueness of a planed surface by placing a straightedge, a combination square or the factory-cut edge of a length of plywood on your board. If any light shows between the board and the straightedge, carefully mark the high spots with a pencil, then plane off your markings.

Although hand planes are relatively simple tools, they are intricately assembled from a number of parts, each with its own distinctive name. Before using a hand plane, remove the iron and familiarize yourself with the parts. The lever cap secures the iron and cap iron in place; all three rest on an angled support called the frog; screws and levers change the depth of the blade, tilt it, or move it forwards and back. With the plane dismantled, sharpen the iron *(pages 90–91)* until it can easily slice through the edge of a piece of paper held in one hand. Then reassemble the parts, taking special care in the precise adjustment of the blade.

The Parts of a Bench Plane

1 **Assembling the iron and cap iron.** Screw the knurled cap screw lightly into the cap iron, then hold the iron, bevel side down, at right angles to the cap iron, slip the head of the cap screw through the hole at the end of the slot of the iron and slide the cap iron at least half way along the slot *(right)*. Rotate the cap iron until the sides of the two irons align—make sure the front of the cap iron does not scrape across the iron's cutting edge. For general work on wood that is fairly easy to cut, such as pine, slide the cap iron forwards gently until the front of its nose is about 2 mm from the edge of the blade. Tighten the cap screw with your fingers, then give it an additional quarter turn with a screwdriver. For wood that is more difficult to cut, such as oak, or for finishing work, advance the cap iron 1 mm closer to the cutting edge.

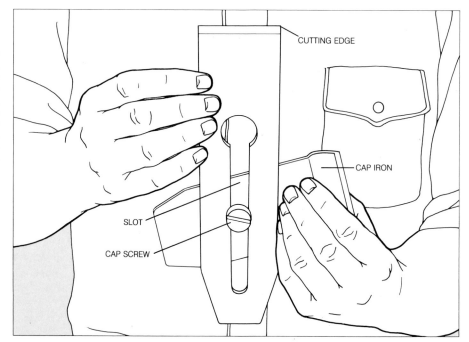

CUTTING EDGE

CAP IRON

SLOT

CAP SCREW

2 **Installing the irons.** Insert the blade into the mouth of the plane, fit the irons over the lever-cap screw, and lay the irons on the frog—the top of the depth-adjusting lug should fit into the window in the cap iron and the lateral-adjusting roller should fit into the iron's slot *(below)*. Set the lever cap on the irons, slide it down until the narrow portion of its hole fits around the lever-cap screw, and snap the lever-cap cam down. The cam should snap down with moderate thumb pressure. If it does not go, release the cam and either loosen the lever-cap screw to decrease tension or tighten it to increase tension.

3 **Setting the depth of the blade.** Hold the plane upright, with the heel resting on a light-coloured surface and the sole facing away from you. Sighting down the sole, turn the depth-adjusting nut until the blade barely protrudes through the mouth; if the blade protrudes farther at one side of the mouth than at the other, use the lateral-adjusting lever to even it.

The mechanical link between the depth-adjusting nut and the depth-adjusting lug has a small amount of play. Make certain that final adjustment of the nut moves the blade deeper through the mouth, otherwise the blade will slide back slightly during the first stroke.

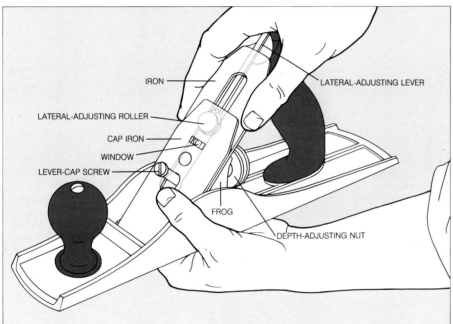

IRON

LATERAL-ADJUSTING LEVER

LATERAL-ADJUSTING ROLLER

CAP IRON

WINDOW

LEVER-CAP SCREW

FROG

DEPTH-ADJUSTING NUT

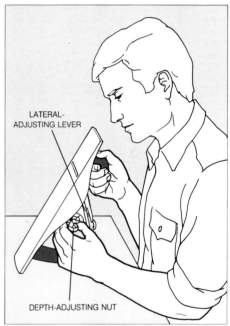

LATERAL-ADJUSTING LEVER

DEPTH-ADJUSTING NUT

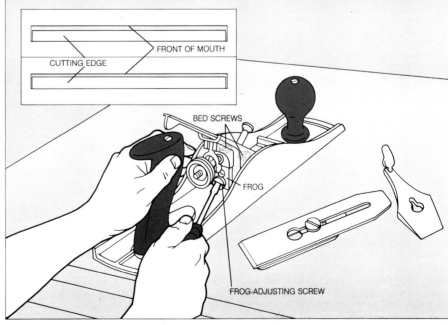

FRONT OF MOUTH

CUTTING EDGE

BED SCREWS

FROG

FROG-ADJUSTING SCREW

4 **Adjusting the mouth.** Turn the sole towards you to check the mouth width. For easy-to-cut wood, use a wide opening; for harder material, use a narrow opening (the inset shows correct widths, actual size). If the opening is too wide or too narrow, remove the lever cap and the irons, exposing two screws called bed screws in the frog. Loosen these, then retract or advance the frog-adjusting screw—only a slight adjustment should be necessary. Reassemble the plane, check the mouth opening again, and test it on a scrap of wood.

Working with the Plane

Planing an edge. Secure the board between two pieces of wood in a vice. Place one hand on the rear handle of the plane, set the toe of the plane squarely on the end of the board and prepare to guide the strokes by curling the other hand round the side of the plane so that your thumb rests near the knob, your fingertips touch the sole just ahead of the blade and the backs of your fingers will brush the board beneath the plane. (If the wood is splintery, guide the plane by placing your forward hand on the knob of the plane.)

Begin the first pass with slightly more pressure on the toe than on the heel. Allow pressure to shift naturally on the plane so that pressure is even in the middle of the pass. To ensure the sole runs flat on the board edge when the blade hits the corner at the end of the stroke, apply slightly more pressure there on the heel.

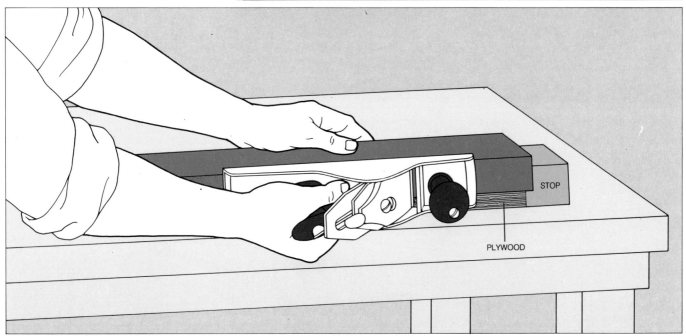

STOP

PLYWOOD

"Shooting" a right angle. To plane the edge of a board perpendicular to its face, place the board on a flat piece of plywood, with the edge of the board overlapping the edge of the plywood by about 3 mm; butt the plywood and the board against a stop fastened to the workbench. Hold the board and the plywood firmly against the stop with one hand, lay the plane, set for a fine shaving, on its side on the workbench and plane towards the stop. Your cuts will result in a perfect right angle since the sole and sides of a plane are milled to meet at 90 degree angles.

If you find it difficult to hold the board steady against a single stop, you may prefer to secure both ends of the board and the plywood base with stops. To shoot several boards in succession, build a permanent shooting board similar to the mitre shooting board shown on page 80, but cut the plywood to the same length as your boards and substitute a perpendicular stop on one end for the mitred stop.

Planing end-grain. Secure the board, end-grain up, in a vice, along with a wood offcut to extend the planing surface beyond the edge of the board. If possible, clamp the offcut to the board so that the planing action cannot cause the two to separate. With the blade set for a very fine cut, place the plane flat on the board as you would in planing an edge, but place the plane itself at about a 30 degree angle with the board. Plane along the board end, holding the plane at the 30 degree angle to slice through the tough end-grain, and continue the strokes on to the offcut.

If you cannot fit the offcut into the vice, plane about three quarters of the way across the end-grain; then, after a few passes, reverse direction by starting the strokes at the opposite side of the board and planing towards, but not over, the portion you have already planed.

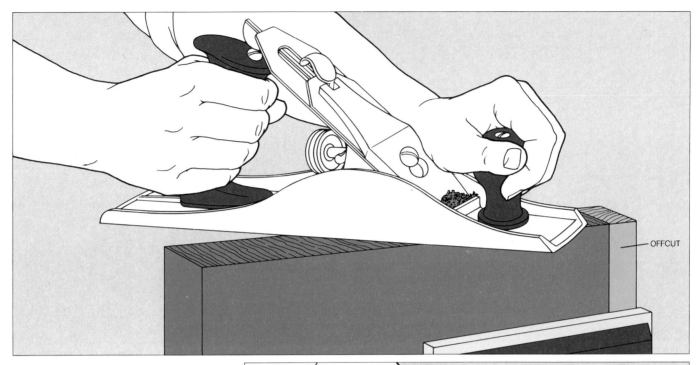

OFFCUT

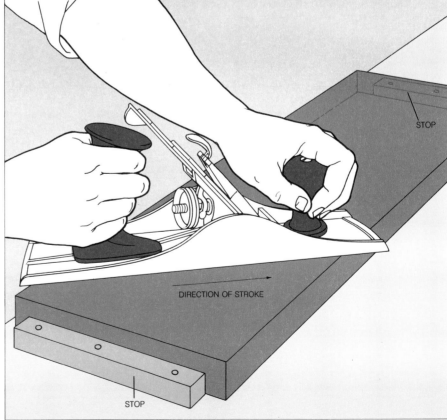

STOP

DIRECTION OF STROKE

STOP

Planing a face. Secure the board between two stops on a workbench, and plane the face in two stages, first for levelling, then for smoothing. In the first stage, set the blade for cuts about as deep as the thickness of an index card; hold the plane at an angle of about 45 degrees to the grain and make straight, slightly overlapping strokes with the edge of the blade at right angles to the direction of the strokes. Before beginning the smoothing stage, resharpen the iron and set the blade for tissue-thin shavings; plane the face with straight strokes parallel to the grain.

Working with a Block Plane

Adjusting the plane. Hold the plane in one hand and use the other to insert the iron, bevel up. Fit the lever cap over the iron and tighten the locking lever. Turn the plane upside down so that you can sight along the sole, then set the depth of the blade with the depth-adjusting nut and set the blade parallel to the sole with the lateral-adjusting lever. For trimming edges on easier-to-cut woods, loosen the finger-rest screw and open the mouth to approximately 1·5 mm by shifting the mouth-adjusting lever; for end-grain, for harder-to-cut woods and for manufactured boards, close the mouth to about 1 mm.

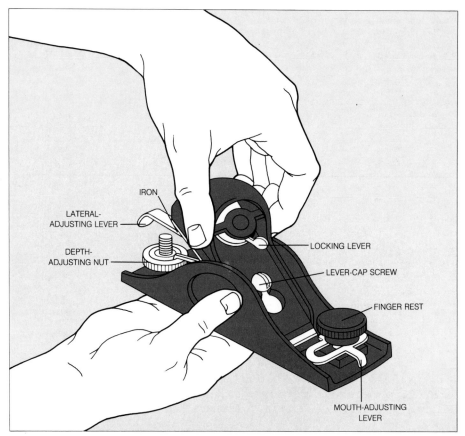

IRON

LATERAL-ADJUSTING LEVER

DEPTH-ADJUSTING NUT

LOCKING LEVER

LEVER-CAP SCREW

FINGER REST

MOUTH-ADJUSTING LEVER

Trimming the wood. Hold the block plane in one hand with your palm on the lever cap, your index finger on the finger rest, and your thumb and fingers on the sides. Begin each stroke with slightly more pressure on the toe, and finish it with slightly more pressure on the heel.

Small chips of wood rather than shavings should rise from end-grain and manufactured boards. If the plane "chatters"—that is, vibrates—and is hard to push, adjust the blade upwards for a shallower cut, and rub beeswax or candlewax on the sole.

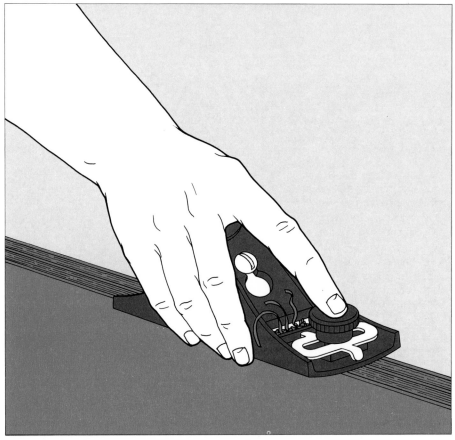

For Big Jobs: a Power Planer

Portable power planes are available in various sizes, ranging from light, 330 watt models with a planing width of 60 mm, to 1,000 watt versions weighing 5 kg and with a planing width of 100 mm. Many come with such accessories as fences and brackets for making square edges and accurate bevels, but all work in much the same way. A rotating cutter block turns at speeds up to 25,000 revolutions per minute, shearing away wood fibre through the plane's mouth. Unlike hand planes, power planes can easily cut across the grain and even against the grain; nevertheless, plane with the grain for best results.

The only adjustment needed on a power plane is depth of the cut, generally regulated by a knob that raises or lowers the toe, which is independent of the rest of the sole; the depth of the blades themselves never changes. In most models, the maximum recommended cutting depth is about 1 mm, a depth suitable for rough wood.

Safety Tips for Power Planers

☐ Fasten the wood securely—in a vice, with cramps, or between strong stops fastened to a workbench.
☐ Keep both your hands on the handles of the plane at all times. Never curl your fingers underneath the sole to guide the plane.
☐ Never set the plane down at the end of a job until the motor has stopped completely.

Setting depth of the cut. With the cord unplugged, turn the adjusting knob; typically, a full turn of the knob raises or lowers the blade about 1 mm. The manufacturer's instructions generally recommend specific depths of cut for various jobs, but make trial cuts on offcuts to be sure you have the depth you need.

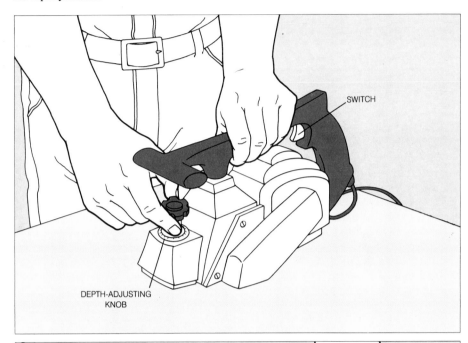

SWITCH

DEPTH-ADJUSTING KNOB

FENCE

Making the cut. Gripping both handles firmly, place the toe of the plane on the board; start the motor while the blades are still clear and let it reach maximum speed before beginning the cut. Move the plane forwards steadily over the board, using more pressure on the toe at the beginning of the cut, and more on the heel at the end of the cut. For smoother cuts, move the plane forwards more slowly.

For such jobs as bevelling or, as in the illustration above, planing the edge of a door, attach a fence to the plane to guide the cut.

Shaving and Shaping to Angles and Curves

Although most boards in a house are squared off all round, some pieces are not. Giving them their final shape requires special techniques and, in a few cases, also special tools. A wooden door edge, for example, is planed to a slanted bevel across the entire width of the edge so that the door closes easily.

A plane, or its relative a spokeshave *(opposite page)*, shapes most edges. Ends cut to a 45 degree angle for a mitre joint may need to be planed to shorten them or to smooth them for a perfect fit, particularly if the joint will have a clear finish and imperfections cannot be hidden by wood filler and paint. This precise planing is simplified with a home-made jig called a mitre shooting board *(page 80, top)*. Also, sharp-edged corners—especially on posts—are relieved by planing just the corner, rather than the entire edge, into a "chamfer".

A decorative variation of the chamfer running only part of the way along the edge is cut with a spokeshave. A spokeshave also finishes edges that curve, although a rasp or glass paper can often serve just as well. For some curved pieces—a curving section of skirting board or a jamb for an arched doorway, for instance—a special procedure must be used to bend a board so that its face curves.

In order to obtain a whole board shaped into a curve, professionals usually bend several thin boards in a large press and glue them together to form a single laminated board of the desired curvature. This technique requires equipment seldom available to amateurs. However, if the piece is less than 25 mm thick, you can bend stock timber by cutting closely spaced saw kerfs part way through the back, then bending and nailing the board round a curved base. Though a kerfed board can be bent round a shallow inside curve—such as the rounded corner of a room—by flexing the kerfs open, the board will bend much farther round an outside curve such as that demonstrated on page 80.

The kerfs that permit bending a board face will show on the edges of the board, and there is no way to conceal them that is both easy and completely satisfactory. Many carpenters fill the edge cuts with wood filler, then sand the edge—a fairly simple job on the squared edge of an arch jamb, but difficult on a skirting board which should have a shaped edge. This problem can be avoided in the case of a skirting board if the curve required is shallow: use plain, square-edged timber for the curving skirting board, then cover the cut edge by nailing to it quadrant or ogee moulding, which is flexible enough to bend somewhat without kerfing.

For a board to be bent in this way, use straight, clear timber, free of knots and cracks. Woods with long fibres—oak, pine and fir, for example—can be bent easily with this method; woods with shorter fibres, such as cherry and mahogany, are stiffer and cannot be bent into extremely tight curves.

Making Bevels and Chamfers with a Bench Plane

Freehand planing at an angle. Using a sliding bevel *(page 26)*, mark the angle of the bevel across the end of the board, then use a combination square and pencil *(page 20)* to mark a line for the bottom of the bevel along the face of the board. Plane the bevel as you would a square edge *(page 74)*, but tilt the sole of the plane roughly parallel to the line on the end of the board. As the plane nears the corner of the board at one face and the line on the opposite face, adjust the angle of the sole precisely, so that you reach both simultaneously. Check the angle of the completed bevel with a sliding bevel and a straightedge, mark any high spots and shave them down.

To flatten a sharp corner over its full length for a "through" chamfer *(inset)*, mark the angle (usually 45 degrees) on the end of the board and mark matching lines on both the face and the edge, then plane the angle as you would a bevel. To make a "stopped" chamfer, which does not run the full length of the corner, use a spokeshave as described on the opposite page.

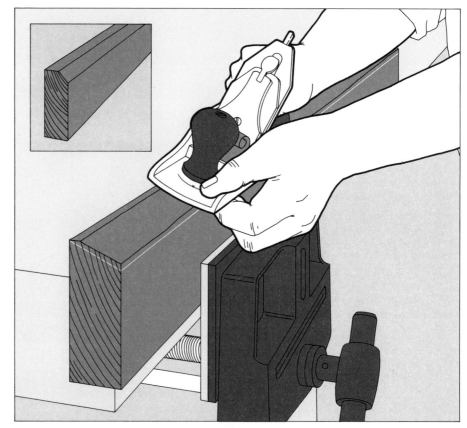

Smoothing Decorative Trim with a Spokeshave

Anatomy of a spokeshave. The parts of a spokeshave fit together in the same way as those of a bench plane, but the spokeshave's short sole—flat for straight and convex shapes, rounded for concave ones—allows it to plane curved surfaces. The blade, bevelled like that of a plane iron *(page 72)*, fits into the body of the spokeshave with its bevel side down. The depth and angle of the blade can be adjusted with flanged nuts that are set in notches in the upper corners of the blade. The blade is held down by an iron lever cap like that of a plane; the fulcrum of the lever is the locking screw that fastens the cap to the body of the spokeshave. The lever cap can be tightened by a knurled thumbscrew that presses against the top of the blade, forcing together the bottom edge of the cap and the blade.

To adjust the blade, tighten the locking screw until it is barely snug, turn the adjusting nuts until the cutting edge of the blade barely projects below the sole, then tighten the thumbscrew firmly by hand. Check the depth adjustment by making trial shavings on an offcut of wood; the wood shavings should be tissue-thin. If the spokeshave vibrates and chops at the wood, reset the blade to a shallower depth.

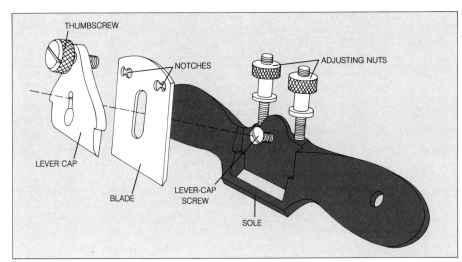

THUMBSCREW
NOTCHES
ADJUSTING NUTS
LEVER CAP
BLADE
LEVER-CAP SCREW
SOLE

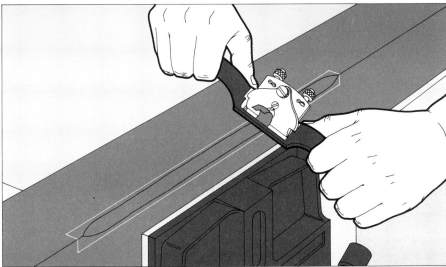

Making a stopped chamfer. Use a pencil and combination square to mark the chamfer lines on the edge and face of the board. Sighting through the mouth, place a flat-bottomed spokeshave on the mark at one end of the chamfer, with the handles tilted 45 degrees from the horizontal. Keeping your wrists slack, push the spokeshave forwards with the grain to a point about 3 mm from the other end. After every two or three passes along the entire length of the chamfer, make a short cut at the far end to pare away the shavings. Shave the chamfer down to the marked lines, then set the blade on the mark at the far end of the chamfer and shave the stop to a smooth, gradual curve that matches the one you made at the starting point.

Smoothing a curve. To finish off a curve that has been cut with a band saw or jigsaw, clamp the board in a vice with the grain running horizontally. Set a spokeshave at the top of a curve and push it slowly to the bottom, using a round-bottomed spokeshave for a concave curve *(above)* and a flat-bottomed one for a convex curve. Then reverse direction and push the spokeshave down from the other side of the curve; work back and forth until the surface is smooth. Do not push the spokeshave uphill, against the grain—it will gouge and chip the surface.

A Shooting Board
for Mitre Cuts

Building a shooting board. Designed to assist in
accurate planing at an angle, this jig has a 450
by 300 mm base of 18 mm plywood, to which is
screwed a 450 by 225 mm shelf and a trapezium-
shaped stop. For one long side of the shelf, use
the straight, factory-cut edge of the plywood, and
attach the shelf so that this straight edge is the
side stepped back from the base.

For the stop, cut a 225 mm rectangle of plywood, then, using a mitre box, cut its ends in two
opposing 45 degree angles about 50 mm apart.
Set the stop on top of the shelf, its 50 mm side
flush with the factory-cut edge. Check its angled
sides with a combination square and move the
stop until they form exact 45 degree angles with
the factory-cut edge, then screw the stop in place.

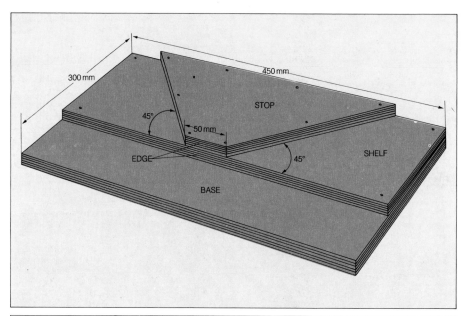

Planing the mitre. Hold the board firmly against
one side of the stop, with the mitred end about
0.5 mm beyond the edge of the stop. Adjust a jack
plane for a very fine cut *(page 73, Step 3)* and rest
it on its side with its toe against the mitre. Slide
the plane forwards repeatedly, starting each
stroke with the toe against the mitre and stop-
ping when the blade passes the mitre—planing
further will plane the trapezium and ruin its
straight edge. As you shave the mitre down, edge
the board forwards so that it always protrudes
about 0.5 mm beyond the stop. If the plane
becomes hard to push, rub beeswax or candlewax
on the shooting board and the side of the plane.

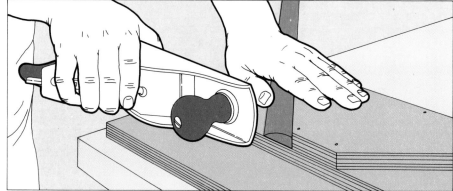

Bending a Board
with the Help of a Saw

Measuring the curve. Hold a straightedge at each
end of the curve and mark the spring lines where
the curve begins *(page 38, Step 2)*. Measure the
distance between the spring lines with a flexible
steel tape and transfer these measurements to
the board you will bend; provide as much unbent
wood at each end of the board as is practical—no
less than 150 mm.

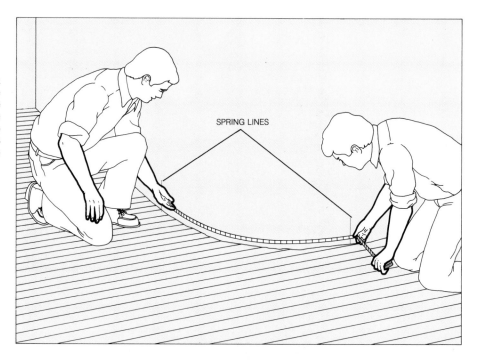

2 **Cutting the kerfs.** You will have to experiment to find the correct depth and spacing of the kerfs for your particular curve and type of wood. If you use a radial arm saw, start by marking the fence 12 mm from the right side of the blade and setting the blade depth 3 mm above the saw table. In a 600 mm offcut that matches the board you plan to bend, cut kerfs at 12 mm intervals *(pages 12–19)*, aligning each new kerf with the mark on the fence for the correct spacing.

Bend the kerfed scrap round a section of the curve to test its flexibility. If you hear cracking in the board or if you have to strain to bend it, make trial cuts in other offcuts, gradually increasing the depth of the cuts and decreasing the space between them until you find the minimum depth and maximum spacing that permits the necessary bend. However, to avoid serious weakening of the wood, you must leave at least 1 mm of uncut wood and space the kerfs at least 6 mm apart. Use the depth and spacing measurements that you determined in the trials on offcuts to make kerfs between the spring lines in the back of the board you plan to bend.

If you use a portable circular saw to cut the kerfs, guide it with the jig shown on page 15, bottom; or mark a line on the board for each kerf, allowing 3 mm for the width of the saw blade, and cut the kerfs freehand.

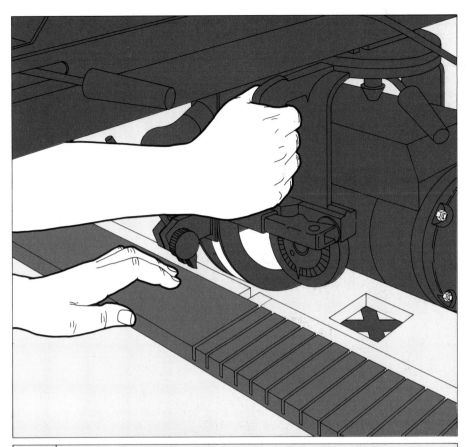

3 **Nailing the kerfed board.** While a helper holds the board—in this example, a section of skirting board—bent around the curve, nail the straight section at one end in the usual way, then drill pilot holes every 200 mm through the uncut wood between kerfs and into the sole plate. Fasten with 63 mm lost-head nails.

To conceal the kerfs exposed at the edge of the board, fill them with wood filler.

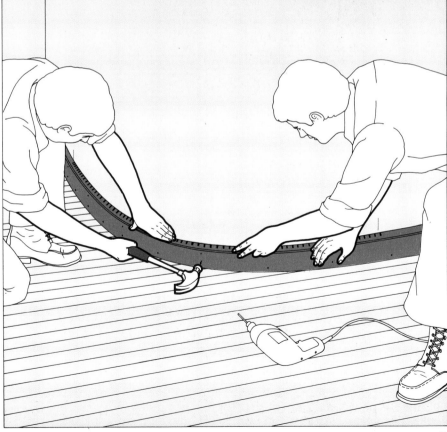

Notches: Rough Passageways and Quick Joints

A multitude of notches must be cut in the timber boards that make up the structural framework of a house or its fittings. There are the passageways that must be cut for the pipes or cables that will run behind the walls or ceilings of finished rooms, and there are the notches that are necessary for joints in, for example, the framework for wall or bath panelling. Since most of these notches will later be concealed by the finished surfaces, you can fashion them roughly—most commonly by making preliminary cuts with a circular saw and then chopping away the wood. The ideal chopping tools for rough notches are firmer chisels with plastic handles and with blades 19 to 25 mm wide.

The techniques for cutting rough notches are simple and quick, but great care must be taken in their planning and placement. Cutting into important structural members such as studs and joists weakens their load-bearing capacity. The cutting of notches in the studs of a load-bearing wall of a timber-frame house is subject to strict building regulations; because the permissible notch size must be calculated separately for each stud, this job is one that is best left to a professional.

Check with your local water authority if you are planning to pass pipework along concealed passageways or notches, as some authorities will only allow either exposed or easily accessible pipes. Notches in non-

load-bearing studs should be kept to a minimum and positioned as closely as possible to the top or bottom of the studs; notches in joists should be positioned as closely as possible to the bearing ends. All notches should be no wider than is necessary to accommodate the pipes or cables that will pass through them. To avoid any danger of nailing into the pipes or cables, protective metal plates should be fitted across the notch openings in chiselled-out recesses *(opposite page, centre)*.

In cases where notches will not be concealed by the finished surfaces of walls, ceilings or panelling, they will require precision cutting such as that demonstrated on pages 64–65 for deep mortises.

Notching the Frame of a House

A shallow V notch in an edge. Turn the bevel of a firmer chisel towards the notch and drive it into the wood at a 45 degree angle to cut one side; then reverse the bevel to chisel in towards the bottom of the first cut, forming the second side. The wood will chip out of the notch as you cut.

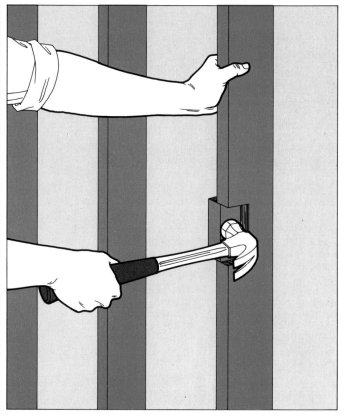

A deep notch in an edge. Set the blade of a circular saw to the depth of the planned notch and make two cuts across the edge of the board to outline the notch; then, with a hammer, strike between the saw cuts to knock out the waste wood with a single sharp blow.

Notching a board face. With a circular saw set to the depth of the required notch, make parallel cuts across the face at each side of the notch and also at approximately 5 mm intervals between the sides. Secure the board, edge up, in a vice. Set the cutting edge of the chisel parallel to the grain and across the inner ends of the saw cuts, with the bevel facing the cuts; then hammer the chisel across the board.

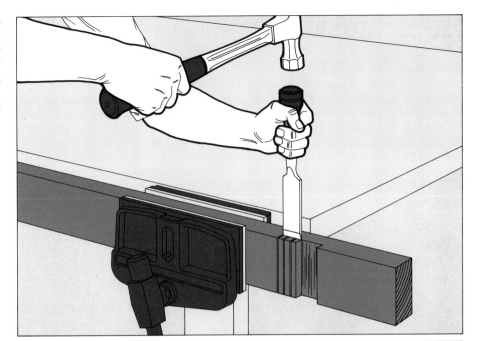

Recessing for a protective plate. Hold a steel plate, which may be needed to protect cable or pipes in a face or edge notch, over the notch and score the wood at the ends of the plate with a trimming knife. Set a firmer chisel perpendicular to the board at each score line, with the bevel facing the notch, and tap the chisel 3 mm deep into the wood *(right)*. To remove the waste wood, set the chisel 3 mm inside the existing notch, with the bevel facing outwards, and drive it to the end of the recess *(far right)*.

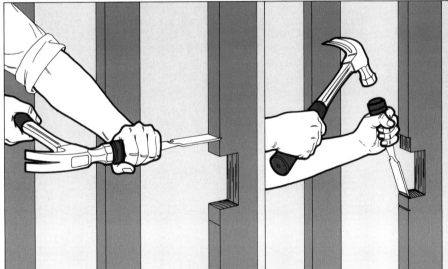

A deep end notch. If the depth of a notch exceeds the maximum depth setting of your circular saw, use the circular saw to cut along marks on the board face as far as the inner corner of the notch. To cut the corner on the underside of the board, where the circular-saw blade did not reach, slide a handsaw into each circular-saw kerf and, holding the cutting edge of the blade vertical, saw the rest of the way to the corner.

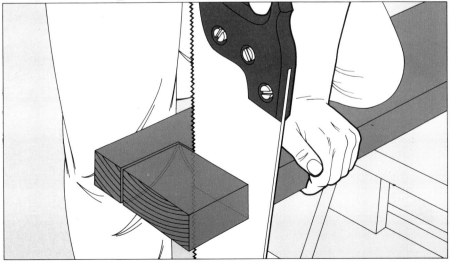

The Ins and Outs of Rebates, Housings and Grooves

The traditional way to make a strong, gap-proof joint between boards—for attaching a fascia board, laying flooring, putting up panelling or finishing stairs—is with an interlocking housing, a groove with its matching tongue, or an overlapping rebate. A rebate is a step cut into the edge of a board; a groove is a channel cut down the length of a board; and a housing is a channel cut across a board. These cuts can be made laboriously and slowly with a saw and chisel, quickly with a router, or very exactly with a radial arm saw.

To rebate a board with a handsaw, make two cuts at right angles to each other along the edge; housing is produced by making several saw cuts spaced as closely as possible to one another within the channel area, then chiselling out the wood; a groove will have to be chiselled out along its length. These hand methods, while quite adequate if you just need to make a few cuts, are time-consuming and tend to be rough. For faster, more precise work, use a router—a power tool designed to cut channels and rebates.

A router requires a guide to keep it cutting in a perfectly straight line. Some rebating bits have built-in ball-bearing guides. Special attachments that fasten to the tool base will guide the cutting at the desired distance from the board edge. But you can make a simple guide yourself from scrap timber and G-cramps. If you want to cut identical rebates or channels in a small number of boards, home-made jigs will guide the router on the boards. However, when construction calls for a variety of cuts in many pieces of timber, the best tool is a radial arm saw equipped with either of two special attachments, a dado headset or a wobbler *(page 87)*.

The Router's Speed: a Mixed Blessing

Routers spin their razor-sharp bits at 22,000 rpm or more—a speed that gives this power tool its advantages of precision and ease of use, but also makes it dangerous.

Fast rotation creates a twisting force that gives the tool a tendency to pull away from its user and expose the sharp cutter. Even after the motor is turned off, the blade does not stop at once.

The high speed of the cutter also makes a router jump if you turn the motor on when the bit is in contact with wood; always keep the bit free when starting up. Handle the router firmly—never gingerly—and use both hands when cutting with it. This is especially important when you are making cuts—such as those with the grain or against the bit's natural tendency to move from left to right—that tend to cause "chatter" or vibration.

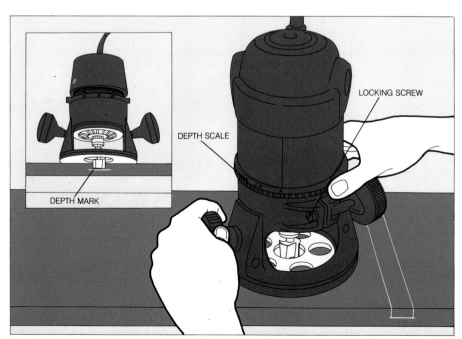

Setting the depth of a cut. Set the router on the board, loosen the locking screw and turn the motor unit clockwise until the tip of the bit just touches the wood; set the depth scale to zero. Move the router bit to the edge of the board and lower the bit until the depth scale registers the desired depth; tighten the locking screw.

To adjust the bit in a router without a depth scale, mark the depth of the desired cut on the side of a board, then turn the motor unit or the depth-adjustment collar to lower the bit until it aligns with the depth mark *(inset)*.

Cut no deeper than 9 mm in one pass; lower the bit and make more passes for deep cuts.

LOCKING SCREW

DEPTH SCALE

DEPTH MARK

Guides for Straight Cuts

A self-guiding rebate bit. This cutter has at its tip a ball-bearing pilot that rolls along the edge of the board and keeps the bit cutting at a uniform width. To use the bit, hold the router with the bit overhanging the edge of the board 50 mm from the left end, turn the motor on and move the bit into the wood until the roller meets the board edge. Move the router from left to right, pressing the guide against the edge *(right)*. Complete the rebate by moving the router from right to left through the uncut edge. Each rebate cutter is designed for one width of rebate but depth is adjustable by the methods described on the opposite page.

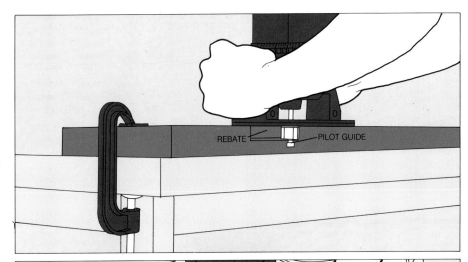

REBATE — PILOT GUIDE

A home-made guide. Clamp a perfectly straight piece of wood to the board to be cut and hold the router firmly against it as you feed the bit through the wood. To determine the position of the guide, first draw lines on the board for the width of the cut. Set the router on top of the board with the bit just above the surface; align the bit with the lines and mark the edge of the router base on the face of the board. Extend the mark across the board with a combination square and clamp the guide along this line.

To rout a board that is narrower than the router's base *(inset)*, clamp a board of equal thickness beside the board to be cut; position a guide board atop this second board and nail through both into the worktable to secure them.

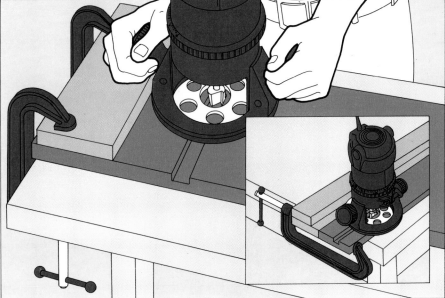

A commercial guide. This edge attachment fastens to the router base; mount it according to the manufacturer's instructions. To use it, measure from the edge of the proposed cut to the edge of the board and set the guide plate that distance from the corresponding edge of the bit; place the guide against the board and keep the two in firm contact as you feed the bit through the wood.

To cut boards narrower than the router's base, clamp boards of equal width on each side of the piece to be cut *(inset)*. Nail a stop board across the side boards at one end to steady the work. Clamp this assembly to the bench.

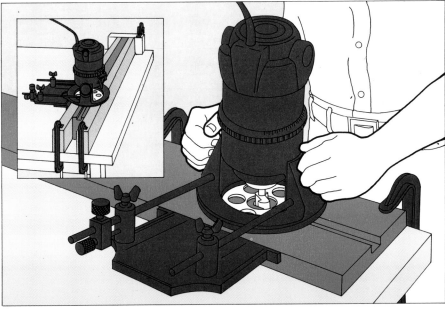

Jigs for Speed and Control

A home-made jig. To cut many straight housings, grooves and rebates in timber of the same dimensions, lay two boards—each 100 mm wide, at least 600 mm long, and the same thickness as the timber to be cut—parallel to each other; space them the width of the timber to be cut. Screw two 50 by 25 mm crosspieces across the boards, spacing them the diameter of the router base; if a wide cut will require more than one pass with the router, add the difference between the width of the proposed cut and the diameter of the bit to the diameter of the base when calculating the spacing of the crosspieces.

Clamp the jig to a workbench, set the bit depth and make a notch the width of the desired cut on the inner edge of each 100 mm board, centring the notches between crosspieces.

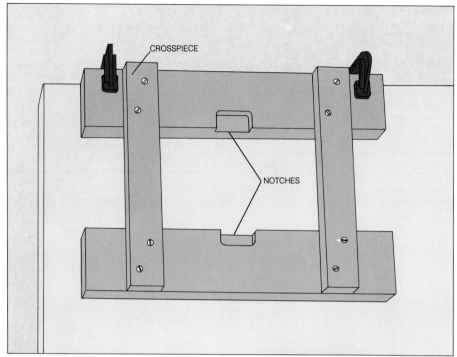

Making straight cuts. Measure and mark the outline on each piece of timber and slide the wood into the jig. Align the marks with the notch edges and nail through the crosspieces to secure the timber temporarily. Set the router bit in one of the jig's notches, turn the motor on and pass the tool steadily along one of the crosspieces to the other notch; for a wide cut like the one illustrated, make a second pass, guiding the router along the second crosspiece.

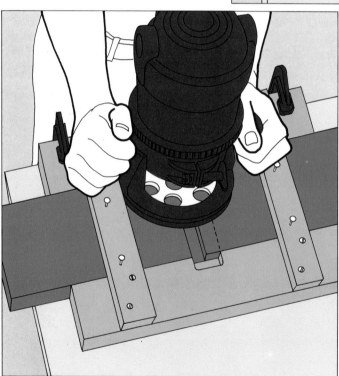

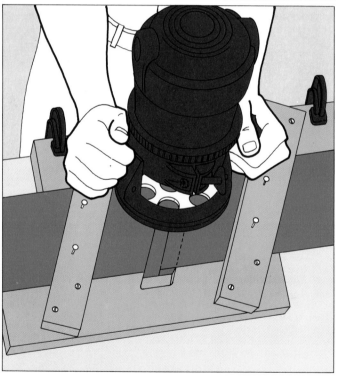

A jig for angles. To cut a housing or groove at an angle or a rebate on an angled end, alter the jig described at the top of this page by setting the crosspieces to the desired angle across the 100 mm boards and providing new or enlarged notches for the router bit. Cut the angles the same way as you make straight cuts.

A jig for stopped cuts. To rout housings, grooves or rebates that do not run completely across a board, alter the jig described opposite by notching only one of the 100 mm boards and adding a 50 by 25 mm stop between the crosspieces. Screw the stop to the unnotched 100 mm board so that the distance from its edge to the inside edge of the desired cut equals the distance from the edge of the bit to the rim of the router base. Follow the technique used for straight cuts, turning the router off when its base hits the stop.

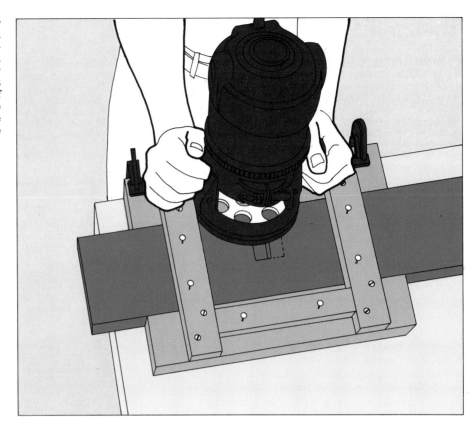

Dado Headset for a Radial Arm Saw

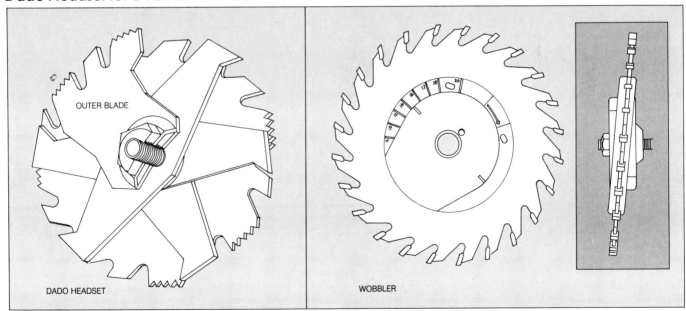

OUTER BLADE

DADO HEADSET

WOBBLER

Two ways to cut a wide path. A radial arm saw can be adapted to cut housings, grooves and rebates efficiently with either of two accessories. The dado headset *(above, left)* replaces the regular blade with two saw blades separated by chippers and an assortment of washers. (Here, the outer blade is largely cut away for clarity.) The width of cut—up to 20 mm—is adjusted by assembling the blades with the appropriate chippers and washers. Less expensive, but also less precise, is the wobbler *(above, right)*—two wedge-shaped washers that grip the regular blade between them, angling it on the axle so that it chews out a wide path *(inset)*. Some wobbler washers are marked so that by turning them you can adjust for a cut as much as 20 mm wide.

Routing a Custom Moulding

Although timber merchants sell a wide selection of mouldings for trimming doors and windows, and to form skirting boards and chair rails, you cannot always find the one you want. But with a router you can produce custom mouldings to suit your own special requirements.

Router bits for shaping decorative edges or grooves come in a large range of styles and sizes that can make cuts as much as 40 mm wide and 20 mm deep. By combining cuts with several bits, you can duplicate or create almost any moulding. To check the cut that will be made by a bit or combination of bits, make test cuts on wood offcuts. Use boards at least 25 mm thick, that are free of knots or warping.

A small amount of moulding can be made by the normal routing technique, but if large amounts are called for—window architraves and skirting for a whole room, for example—convert your router into a home-made spindle *(opposite page)* by mounting it on a simple wooden table, which enables you to repeat the same cut accurately in several pieces of wood. Mount the router upside down under the table and mount the table on a workbench, or alternatively clamp it to sawhorses, then adjust the router-bit depth and the table fence for your cut.

Since the router's rotating bit is exposed above the table surface, be scrupulous about safety precautions. Keep hands well away from the moving bit and use push sticks to finish cuts. To make sure you can shut the tool off quickly and safely, power the router from a switched socket outlet mounted on the worktable; connect the outlet to your power source with three-core cable and an earthed plug.

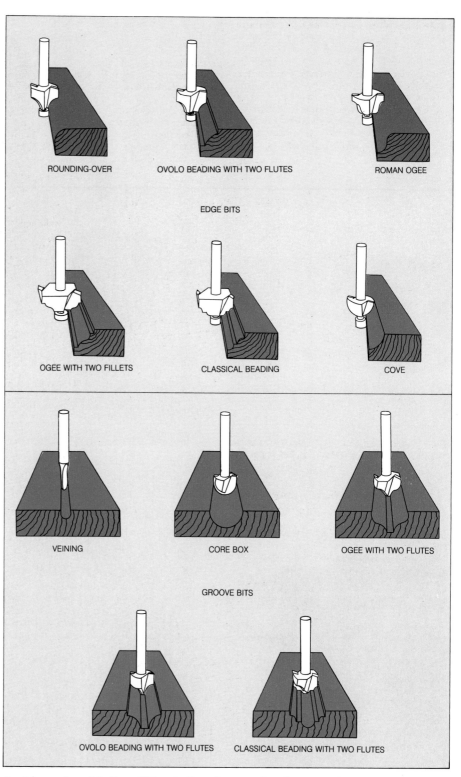

EDGE BITS

ROUNDING-OVER · OVOLO BEADING WITH TWO FLUTES · ROMAN OGEE

OGEE WITH TWO FILLETS · CLASSICAL BEADING · COVE

GROOVE BITS

VEINING · CORE BOX · OGEE WITH TWO FLUTES

OVOLO BEADING WITH TWO FLUTES · CLASSICAL BEADING WITH TWO FLUTES

A catalogue of special effects. This selection of router bits represents only a fraction of the profiles to choose from for forming edges and grooves. Edging bits generally have ball-bearing pilot guides that ride along the side of a board to help position the router. The width of any cut is limited by the width of the bit, but bits can be used in combination to create wider designs; for example, a deep cut with a core-box bit next to a shallow cut with a rounding-over bit would produce an ogee curve wider than the one that an ogee bit used alone can produce. The router's depth of cut is adjustable and some cutters, such as the ogee edging bit with two fillets, can produce more than one profile, depending on the depth to which the router is set.

A Router Table for Mass Production

Building a router table. Fasten 200 by 50 mm timber legs on opposite sides of a 750 mm square of 18 mm plywood with four countersunk wood screws. Locate the board's centre by drawing diagonal lines from corner to corner and drill a hole 3 mm wider than the widest bit you plan to use. With the router's base removed, centre the tool over the bit hole and mark the location of the screw holes in the base. Drill and countersink holes for the machine screws that will hold the router upside down under the table. For safety and convenience, plug the router cord into a switched socket mounted on the table.

Make a fence that is the same length as the table, using a perfectly straight piece of 50 by 25 mm timber. In the centre of one side of the fence, cut a semi-circular notch to match the table's bit hole. Use G-cramps to hold the fence to the table; you will then be able to move the fence to accommodate boards of any width. When using the router to shape narrow edges *(bottom left)*, construct a triangular or rectangular plywood push-frame with a batten along one side to help you to keep the timber correctly aligned.

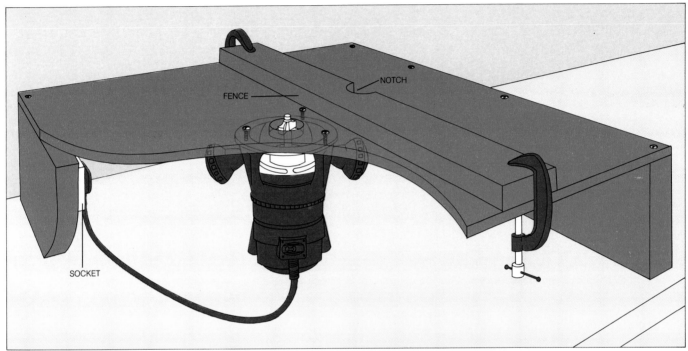

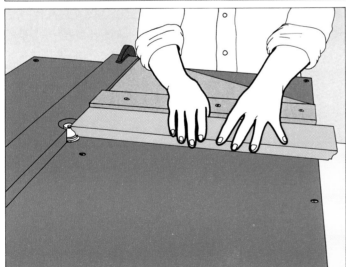

Shaping edges. Align the notched side of the fence over the bit hole and, with the bit rotating anticlockwise into the wood, use a push-frame to guide the timber into and past the bit. Hold the wood firmly against both the table and the fence and keep your hands well away from the bit.

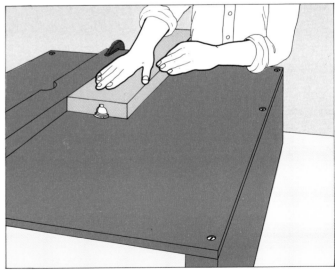

Shaping a groove. Position the fence so that its distance from the bit is the same as that from the board edge to the required groove. Clamp the fence to the table with the straight edge towards the cutter, and adjust the bit depth as necessary. Push the board slowly over the bit, holding the wood firmly against the fence.

Sharpening a Shaper to a Fine Cutting Edge

When a cutting tool that is used to remove thin parings of wood requires more than light pressure to do its job, its edge needs to be renewed; it should be sharpened by honing and stropping. If a cutting edge is nicked or the bevel leading to the edge has become thickened or rounded, the blade must be reshaped with a grinding wheel.

The shape of the cutting edge determines how it is honed. Tools with straight blades and edges, such as plane irons, wood chisels and some drawknives and axes, are honed by rubbing the bevelled edge of the blade against oilstones—first medium grit, then finer grit—set on a flat surface. The burr, or wire edge, created by honing is removed by rubbing the flat side of the blade on a fine-grit oilstone.

Tools with edges that curve outwards, such as adzes and some axes used for rough carpentry, are sharpened with an oilstone held in the hand. Tools with blades that are curved in cross-section—such as gouges, curved chisels and some drawknives—are trickier. The bevelled outside curve of the blade is honed by rubbing it against an oilstone lying on a flat surface; the flat inside curve is honed with a slipstone—a small, wedge-shaped stone having one rounded edge—held in the hand.

To accomplish these honing operations, a variety of oilstones are available. Natural stones made of the mineral novaculite—called Washita stones in medium grit, Arkansas stones in fine grit—cut slowly but produce an extremely keen edge that stays sharp longer than one honed on an artificial stone. Considerably less expensive than natural stones, artificial stones are made of either aluminium oxide or silicon carbide. Stones of silicon carbide cut faster, while aluminium oxide stones give a sharper edge. Most versatile are combination man-made stones, medium grit on one side, fine on the other side.

Soak new stones overnight in mineral oil or a lightweight machine oil. Before each use, apply a light coating of oil; after use, wipe with a clean cloth. Store in containers—wooden boxes are common—to keep them clean and safe from breakage.

To complete a sharpening operation, strop a blade on a piece of smooth leather that has been rubbed with a little oil, jeweller's rouge or emery powder. Honed tools should slice cleanly through paper or shave the hair on your arm.

If a tool requires more than sharpening and has to be reshaped to eliminate nicks and correct the bevel, use a grinder, generally with a medium-fine 60-grit or 100-grit vitrified aluminium oxide wheel. Follow the manufacturer's recommendations for the operation of your grinder and observe the safety precautions for grinders (box, page 67)—because of their high speed of rotation, they can throw off fragments with killing force. Cut metal from the edge, working slowly, and dip the tool in water frequently to cool it. Overheating the metal will draw its temper, so that it will not take a sharp edge.

Careful storage can minimize the kinds of damage that lead to regrinding. Hang tools in racks, sheathe them in leather or keep them in canvas rolls. Oil each edge lightly after each use to inhibit rust. Store a plane on its side, with the iron retracted so that it does not protrude through the sole plate; store cutters or blades for power tools in their protective cases.

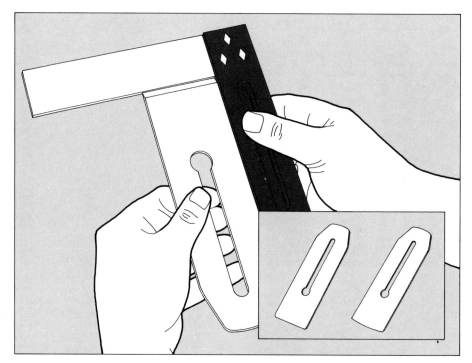

Straight-edged shapers. Use a try square to check the edge of any wood chisel or the iron of a block plane designed for precise cuts; the edges should be perfectly straight and should have perfectly square corners. The corners of a plane iron designed for general-purpose work should be slightly rounded *(inset, left)*. The iron of a jack or jointer plane, designed for the fast removal of larger amounts of wood, is ground with a slightly convex edge *(inset, right)*, the centre about 1 mm higher than the corners.

Curved shapers. Trace the curved silhouette of an axe or adze and use the tracing as a template when reshaping damaged edges. The cutting edge of a firmer gouge, like that of a chisel or a plane iron, is perpendicular to the tool's blade; the blade itself is curved and is bevelled on the outside of the curve *(inset)*.

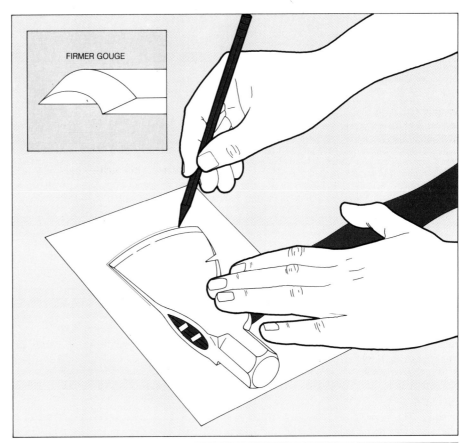

FIRMER GOUGE

Bevel angles. Use a protractor bevel, which combines the features of a protractor and a sliding bevel, in order to measure the angle of a tool's bevelled edge when grinding the tool. The bevels of chisels, gouges, plane irons and drawknives are hollowed slightly by a grinding wheel *(inset, left)*; the bevels should be twice as long as the thickness of the blades and should be cut at a 25 degree angle to the flat side of the blade. (Chisels used for precision cuts or easier-to-cut woods are sometimes ground to a 15 or 20 degree angle, but these thin edges are especially susceptible to nicking.) Axes are ground with slightly convex bevels for greater strength *(inset, centre and right)*. Some have only one bevel, ground at a 25 degree angle; others are double-bevelled, with the two bevels at a 30 degree angle.

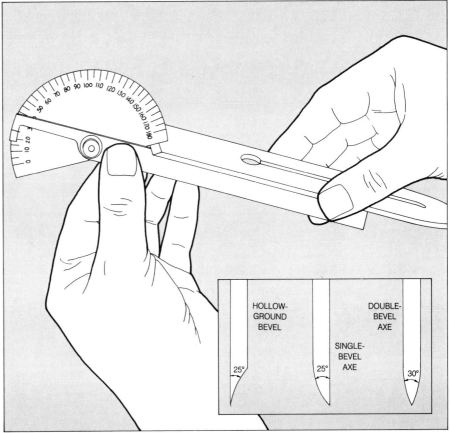

HOLLOW-GROUND BEVEL

DOUBLE-BEVEL AXE

SINGLE-BEVEL AXE

25°   25°   30°

Honing a Straight Edge

1 Positioning the bevel. Standing with your feet slightly apart, grip the tool comfortably and lay its bevel flat against a medium-grit oilstone; hold the bevel lightly against the oilstone with the fingers of your free hand. Brace your lower forearm firmly against your body and stiffen the wrist of the hand holding the tool to maintain the angle of the bevel as it rests on the stone.

If you find it hard to brace the tool on the stone, use a honing jig *(inset)* to hold chisels or plane irons at the correct angle.

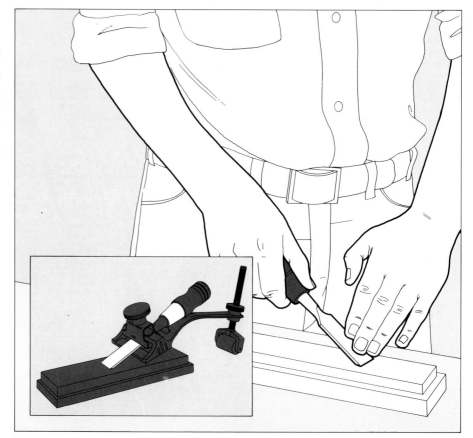

2 Sharpening the bevel. Rock your body in small circles from the ankles, so that the bevel moves in small circles or ellipses; with a honing jig, make straight push-pull strokes. Exert pressure on the circular or straight pulling strokes; use the pushing ones to reposition the bevel for the next stroke. Keep the bevel flat on the stone—rocking it will dull the edge or round the bevel.

When you have worn a uniform, dull-grey scratch pattern across the bevel and no shiny spots show along the edge, repeat Steps 1 and 2 on a fine oilstone until you can feel a burr, or wire edge *(inset)*, when you run a finger up the flat side of the blade and past the edge.

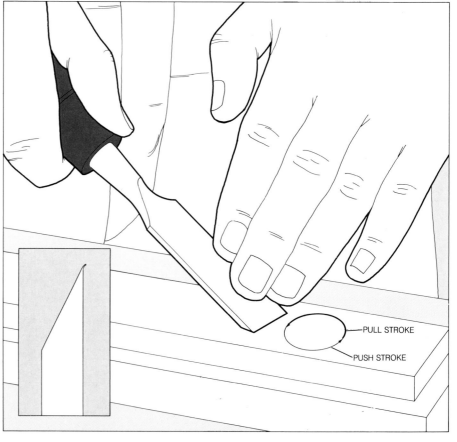

PULL STROKE

PUSH STROKE

3 **Removing the wire edge.** Turn the blade over, hold it flat against a fine oilstone and pull the blade repeatedly along the length of the stone until you can no longer feel the wire edge. Finish honing with pulling strokes on a leather strop, on both the flat and bevelled sides of the blade.

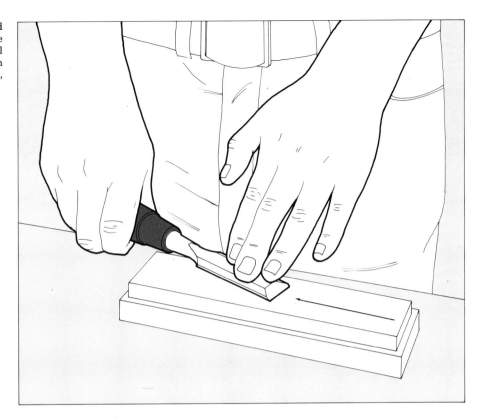

Honing and Stoning a Curved Edge

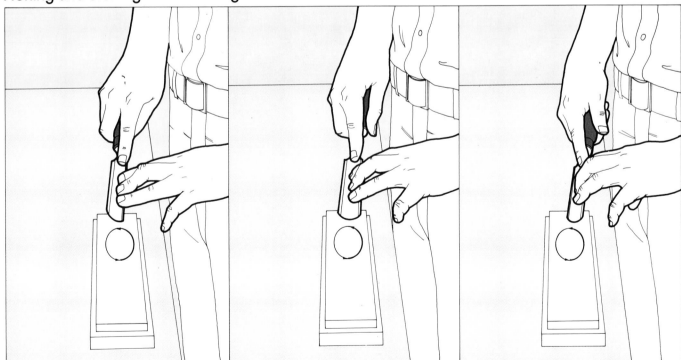

1 **Honing a firmer gouge.** Hold the tool and sharpen it as described in Steps 1 and 2 *(opposite page)*, but roll the tool from side to side as you work. Start on one side of the curved edge *(above, left)*, and move the bevel in several circles; roll the tool slightly, and hone the middle of the bevel *(above, centre)*, then roll it again to hone the opposite side *(above, right)*. Repeat rolling and honing until the entire surface of the bevel has a uniform scratch pattern.

2 **Removing the wire edge from a curve.** Hold the curved edge of a slipstone flat against the inside of a firmer-gouge blade and slide the stone back and forth; repeat the strokes along the entire edge, always keeping the slipstone flat against the blade, until the wire edge has been removed.

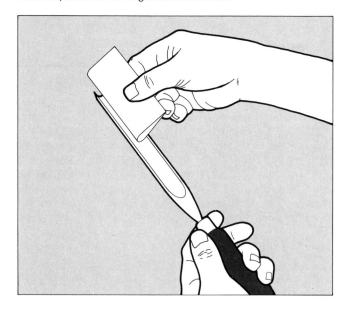

Sharpening a Convex Bevel

Honing an axe. Hold a coarse or medium oilstone against the very edge of the axe's convex bevel; do not hold the stone flat against the bevel or you will deform the bevel shape. Move the stone along the edge in small circles, then repeat the process with a finer stone. On a double-bevelled blade, honing both bevels will remove the wire edge. If the blade has a single bevel, remove the wire edge from the flat side with an oilstone (*page 93, Step 3*).

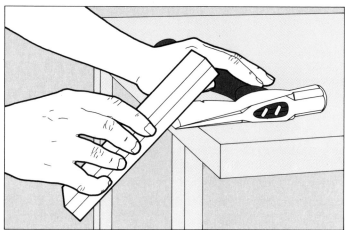

Restoring a Hollow Bevel with a Grinding Wheel

1 **Setting the tool rest.** Loosen the wing nut of the tool rest and adjust the rest so that, with the tool flat against it, the tool bevel meets the face of the grinding wheel at the correct angle and at a point above the wheel axis. The tool rest should be as close as possible to the wheel to avoid any risk of the tool falling into the gap between the rest and the wheel.

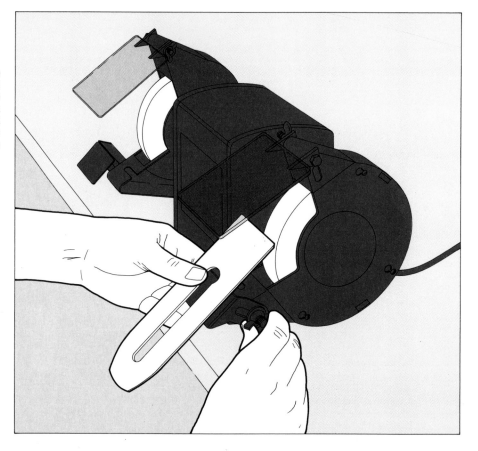

2 **Grinding the bevel.** With the grinder on, bring the edge of the tool into light contact with the circumference of the wheel. If you are grinding a straight-edged tool, move it back and forth across the circumference; if you are grinding a firmer gouge, roll it to present all parts of the bevel to the wheel. Make light cuts and cool the blade frequently in water. Use a protractor bevel repeatedly to check the angle as you grind it. When the bevel is held to strong light, you should see a uniformly shiny scratch pattern; a patchy surface with both shiny and dull spots indicates an unevenly ground bevel.

Restoring a Convex Bevel

Freehand grinding. Hold the heel of a convex bevel against the grinding wheel and pass the blade across the circumference; if the tool has a curved edge, like the one on the right, move it in a small arc to keep the heel of the bevel against the wheel. Before making the next pass across the wheel, raise the heel slightly and rock the edge forwards; repeat this procedure until the edge of the bevel passes across the wheel. Cool the blade frequently, check the angle with a protractor bevel, and check the outline of a curved edge against your tracing of it *(page 91, top)*.

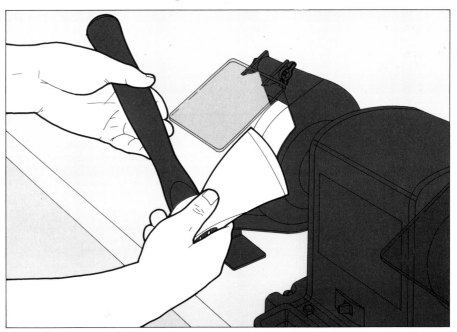

4

Making Perfect Joints

Until the last century, houses were put together by the ancient art of joinery. One end or edge of a piece of wood was shaped to fit into a mating shape in the end of another piece. The two pieces interlocked like the parts of a jigsaw puzzle, and the stresses of weight, wind and movement, which act to pull apart the elements of a house, were resisted by the shapes of the wood. There were no nails; they were too costly to use for the routine purpose of fastening together parts of a house.

The machine age changed this way of building; metal, not sculpted ends, began to hold together most of the wood in a house. Steel, which had been costly, became plentiful and cheap. Nails no longer had to be forged and cut by hand but could now be mass-produced by the machines that spun out threads of steel and readily chopped them to any length. Over the decades, a bewildering array of metal fasteners has been developed to make flat-faced connections strong and neat, thus saving the time and painstaking labour of sculpting wood ends and edges into interlocking shapes.

There are screws for joints that have to be extra strong, bolts for fastening timbers, and corrugated or toothed fasteners to hold delicate pieces of wood *(pages 98–99)*. For heavier joints, metal is shaped into framing anchors that strap joists and rafters into place. There are special hardened nails for fastening wood to bricks and concrete, while others have spiral shanks to increase their surface area and create more friction with the wood.

Yet for all the versatility of metal fasteners, some wood-shaped joints have survived—and are used today for the same reason that they were developed hundreds of years ago: they hold better. Their extra grip is needed where a small, weak joint, if rigidly connected, might work loose under repeatedly varying loads of changing stresses. Most are factory-made, in parts bought assembled from a mill, and demand attention only if they need to be reglued or, in rare instances, repaired with a hand-cut replacement part.

The top of a door lining, for example, is stepped into the jambs in a rebate joint, to help resist the twisting force of door slams *(page 114)*. In window sashes and doors, mortise and tenon joints *(opposite)* hold against repeated pushes and pulls *(pages 118–123)*. Stair treads and risers are made with grooved joints to counter the shifting weight of the people using them *(page 115)*. In these and several other joints around the house, metal fasteners must take a secondary role: the skills of the old carpenters, the beauty of shaped wood, and the strength of wood bearing on wood have survived the advances of the machine age.

An Arsenal of Specialized Metal Fasteners

Most joints in wood rely on metal fasteners. Although some joints are held together by glue and others are made from parts that interlock, nails, screws, bolts and a host of specialized steel connectors give woodworkers the fastest, most efficient means of joining timber. So many of these metal fasteners have been devised that choosing the correct one for a specific job can be difficult. The decision must take into account the strength needed for the joint, the possibility that it may have to be unfastened at a later time and the importance of its appearance.

Nails, the most common fasteners, are quick, easy and inexpensive. Like all metal fasteners, they work by friction: a driven nail displaces wood fibres, which clamp the shank in place. However, nails with long, sharp points, though they enter the wood easily, may split the fibres apart. Blunt-pointed nails, which can be either factory-made or blunted on the job, hold rather better because the blunt point clears a path through the wood and leaves a tight sleeve of unsplit fibres round the shank.

Once a nail is in place, two kinds of force can dislodge it. One kind, shearing stress, is exerted at an angle perpendicular to the shank. The other, withdrawal stress, is applied parallel and opposite to the direction of entry. A nail withstands shearing stress better than withdrawal stress, and should be driven across the grain, so that the main force against it, once the nail is in place, is shearing force.

Screws have greater holding power than nails do against withdrawal stress because their threads present a larger surface area, which creates greater friction with the wood fibres. What is more, they are easy to remove without splintering or gouging wood. But they are more expensive than nails and take more time to install. Before you can screw two pieces of wood together, you will need to drill one or more pilot holes *(page 105)*.

Nuts and bolts are less commonly used than nails and screws, because both ends of the bolt must be accessible, an impossibility in many situations; but they do form exceptionally tight, strong joints between pieces that are too large for the common fasteners. Still other fasteners are relatively specialized. For fine work that is to be covered, corrugated or toothed fasteners make tight joints where nails or screws would split the wood, as in frames for flush doors. In rough construction, shaped metal plates called anchors or framing connectors secure structural members.

Glues, though more common in cabinet-making than in house carpentry, add to the strength of any metal fastener. Epoxy resin, casein glue and synthetic resin glue are all commonly used in joining wood.

From Common Nails to Nuts and Bolts

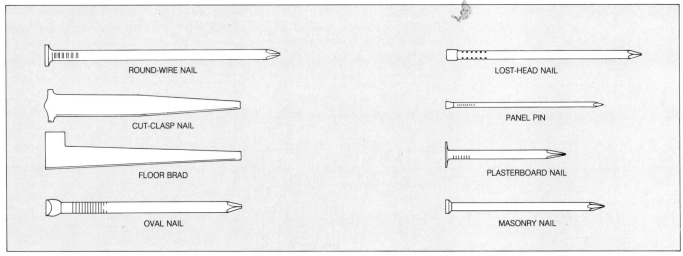

ROUND-WIRE NAIL

CUT-CLASP NAIL

FLOOR BRAD

OVAL NAIL

LOST-HEAD NAIL

PANEL PIN

PLASTERBOARD NAIL

MASONRY NAIL

Nails. Round-wire nails, also known as French nails, are used in general construction work where the surface appearance is not important, such as roofing, studwork and carcassing. Cut-clasp nails and floor brads are wedge-shaped, which gives them great holding power. Cut-clasps are used for fixing door and window linings and skirting boards to masonry supports such as breeze and insulation blocks. Floor brads are traditionally used for fixing plain square-edged or tongue and groove floorboards. They can be removed easily.

Oval and lost-head nails are used in joinery work and fixing mouldings. The elliptical head and shaft of the oval nail minimize splitting; the head of the lost-head nail, which is the same diameter as the shank, is easily punched below the wood surface. Panel pins are suitable for fixing delicate mouldings and for work with thin materials, such as boxing in pipes with hardboard or plywood. Three types are available—plain, deep drive and veneer.

Plasterboard nails—known as clout nails when under 25 mm long—have large heads for fixing plasterboard to ceiling joists and wall studs, and are zinc coated to prevent rusting. Masonry nails, used for fixing wood on to concrete and brickwork, are liable to break if not hit squarely; goggles should be worn as a protection against flying bits of broken masonry.

With the exception of masonry nails, which are sold by number, nails are sold by weight. They are available in a range of sizes from 25 to 100 mm long. For special work, round-wire and cut-clasp nails up to 200 mm in length can be bought. Panel pins range from 12 to 50 mm.

Screws. Screws for woodworking all have sharp threads that taper to a point. They differ in size, head shape and slotting, and some no longer have the traditional smooth shank.

Coach screws are the largest and are used for heavy work. Their square or hexagonal heads are turned by wrenches; some have slots so they can be turned by screwdrivers as well. Coach screws are measured in millimetres for both length and diameter.

Standard wood screws—those with smooth shanks and slotted heads—are most commonly available in three head shapes and slot types. Countersunk screws are the most common because they are easily countersunk either flush with the surface or below it and covered with filler. Raised and countersunk screws and round-heads generally are left exposed for decorative effect. Single, crosshead and Posidriv slots are equally common, but a Posidriv head gives the best control. Always use the appropriate screwdriver for each slot. Standard screws are sized by diameter in gauge numbers and by length in millimetres—common gauge numbers are 6, 8, 10 and 12.

Self-tapping screws, which have threads extending to the heads, are used especially for attaching plywood panels and hardware. They come in the three common head shapes plus a fourth called a pan-head, and have either crosshead or single slots. They are sized like standard wood screws. Twinfast chipboard screws have parallel-sided rather than tapered shanks which chipboard grips better. The double twist enables them to be screwed in faster than single twist shanks.

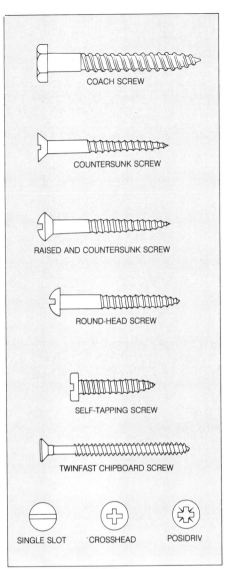

COACH SCREW

COUNTERSUNK SCREW

RAISED AND COUNTERSUNK SCREW

ROUND-HEAD SCREW

SELF-TAPPING SCREW

TWINFAST CHIPBOARD SCREW

SINGLE SLOT   CROSSHEAD   POSIDRIV

Bolts. Though most common in metalwork, bolts, washers and nuts have important uses in wood construction. Handrail bolts, the most specialized, join both curved and straight handrails. Machine screws are used to join 100 by 50 mm boards for rough shelving; machine and carriage bolts, which are stronger and heavier, are used in fixing timber to steelwork.

Bolts are sized by diameter of the thread and by length from the bottom of the head to the end of the bolt. Flat-head machine screws, however, are measured from the top of the head.

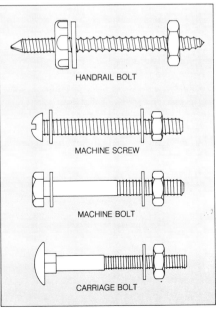

HANDRAIL BOLT

MACHINE SCREW

MACHINE BOLT

CARRIAGE BOLT

Anchors. Framing anchors are designed for a variety of connections. They are increasingly popular because they eliminate toenailing and difficult hammering angles. An anchor is fastened to wood by 40 mm round-wire nails or by spiral-shanked nails packaged with the anchor.

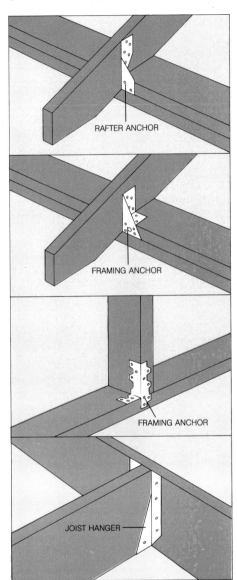

RAFTER ANCHOR

FRAMING ANCHOR

FRAMING ANCHOR

JOIST HANGER

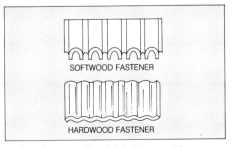

SOFTWOOD FASTENER

HARDWOOD FASTENER

Finishing fasteners. Special fasteners with corrugated edges or projecting teeth reinforce weak joints between butted pieces, such as frames for flush doors and panelled baths.

How a Pro Hammers a Nail

The first hard lesson every amateur carpenter learns is the difficulty of driving a nail straight and true. The skill of the professional comes only with practice, but some basic facts make expertise easier to acquire. You need to know how to choose a hammer, how to set the nail at the proper angle and how to adjust your swing to the location of the nail. Even pulling nails involves special techniques.

Good nailing begins with the right hammer. The ones used in carpentry come with different heads and in several weights. The two most useful hammers are the claw and the cross-pein, or Warrington.

The claw hammer is the most widely used because it serves as a general purpose tool. The claw may be curved or straight. The curved type, more common in house carpentry, is better for pulling nails because its head can roll back further with a nail in its grip. The straight-claw hammer is used mainly for framing and renovation work; its claw wedges more easily between boards to prise them apart. Some straight-claw hammers—and a few curved-claw models—have a cross-checked face that reduces the tendency of the face to slip off a nail, but leaves a checked pattern on the wood surface.

A 500 g claw hammer can be used for finish as well as framing, and is the preferred weight for general use; the other common size, 600 g, is used for heavier work such as hammering nails over 100 mm long.

The cross-pein hammer has a tapered pein which is used for starting nails held between the fingers. A lightweight hammer—250 g to 450 g—is best for finish work, as it is less likely to damage the wood.

Handles are available in wood, steel and glass fibre, but choosing among them depends less on a specific job than on feel and ease of maintenance. Wooden handles will absorb more of the shock of hammering, but eventually loosen and need retightening (right). Steel and glass fibre handles rarely come loose, but both vibrate badly when driving large nails; of the two, glass fibre is lighter but occasionally breaks, while steel is almost indestructible.

Nailing technique varies, not with the type of hammer but with the way the nail is to be driven—into a board face, at an angle for toenailing, or straight through and bent over for clench-nailing. If you do bend a nail or drive it wrongly, do not try to straighten it—simply pull it out and drive a new one. The claws of a hammer will do the pulling job well enough; but such tools as pincers, a nail bar and a nail puller *(page 104)* make the job faster.

Never forget that hammering is hard on muscles and bones. Carpenters fall prey to the same ailments that affect tennis players. If, while working, you feel pain in an arm or shoulder, stop immediately.

Tightening a wooden handle. Use a cold chisel to make a groove 1 mm deep in the top of the handle, half way between and parallel with the fastening wedges already inserted in the handle top at the factory. Set a new wedge, sold at ironmongers, into the groove and drive it into the handle with a cross-pein hammer until the wedge barely moves with each blow; if you drive it further you may split the handle. Using a hacksaw, cut the protruding portion of the wedge flush with the top of the hammer head.

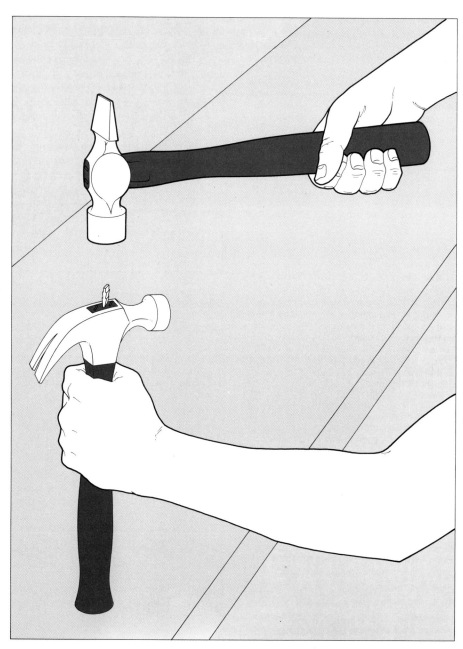

Starting the nail. Hold the nail near its tip between your thumb and index finger, angle it about 10 degrees from you—it will straighten under the hammer blows—and tap it lightly. Support the nail with your fingers until it is driven deep enough into the wood to stand by itself.

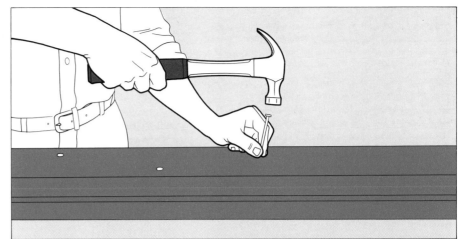

Driving the nail home. Swing the hammer up to shoulder level; deliver the blow using a strong wrist action. When the hammer strikes the nail, its handle should be at a 90 degree angle with the nail shaft, and the nail head directly below the centre of its face. Adjust the force of the last blow to drive the head of the nail flush with the wood surface.

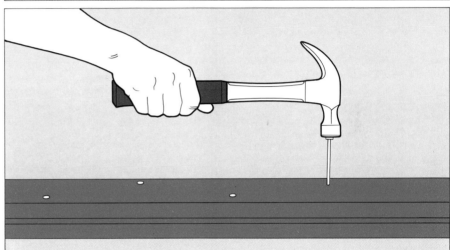

Nailing out. If you have to nail a joint located between knee and shoulder height in a space too restricted for a normal swing, nail horizontally in front of your body, using a stroke called nailing out. Grip the hammer with your thumb on the back of the handle for better control. Hold the hammer with its head in front of you, bend your arm back towards your body and drive the nail by swinging your arm outwards.

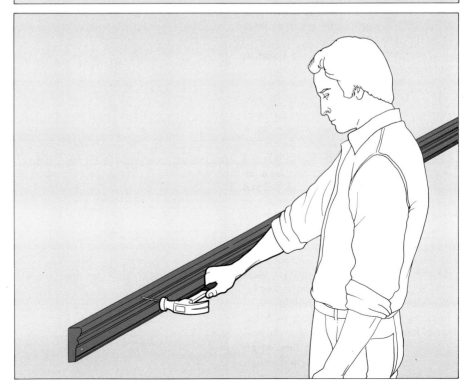

Nailing up. When the joint you are nailing is above your head, grip the hammer as you would for nailing out *(page 101, bottom)* and swing your arm upwards with a full wrist and lower arm motion. If the work is so high that your arm would be almost fully extended at the end of the swing and the hammer cannot hit the nail squarely, stand on a ladder so that your striking position resembles that shown on the right.

Toenailing. To brace the board being toenailed, drive a nail at a 70 degree angle part way into the joint between two pieces; to make a check in the accuracy of the final toenails, draw a short straight line along the middle of the piece being toenailed and on to the second piece. Locate the starting point of the first toenail so that one-third of the nail, if driven at a 45 degree angle, will lie in the piece being toenailed and two-thirds in the second piece; for a 75 mm wire nail driven into 100 by 50 mm boards, this point is about 25 mm from the end of the piece being toenailed. Start the nail at a 90 degree angle *(right, top)*; when you have driven it about 10 mm into the wood, tip it up about 45 degrees and drive it in at that angle *(right, bottom)* until its head dents the wood. If a second nail is needed, drive it in in the same way.

Remove the bracing nail and toenail the pieces together on the other side. Check the pencil line; if its two parts have been displaced, hammer one side of the toenailed piece to bring the lines together. In rough framing an error of 6 mm is generally acceptable.

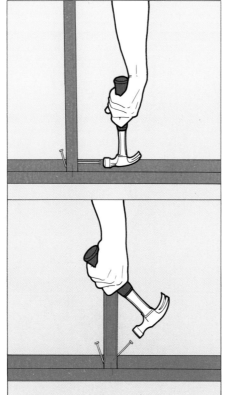

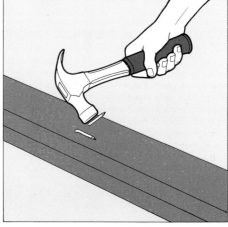

Clench-nailing. To make a support post or a composite header above a door by doubling boards, place the boards face to face and drive through them nails 30 per cent longer than their combined thickness. Drive the nail heads flush, turn the pieces over, set them on a hard, flat surface and hammer the projecting nail shanks at an angle, bending them as close to the surface as possible. Align the shanks with the grain for a smoother surface, but across the grain for a stronger joint. When the shanks are nearly horizontal, strike them with two or three vertical blows to seat them deeply in the wood.

Driving and Punching
a Lost-Head or Oval Nail

1 **Starting the nail.** Hold the nail as you would for rough work *(page 101, top)*, but wrap your fingers round the hammer handle and set your thumb along the handle as shown. Hit the nail lightly, supporting it with your fingers until it can stand by itself, then driving it until its head is about 3 mm above the surface of the wood.

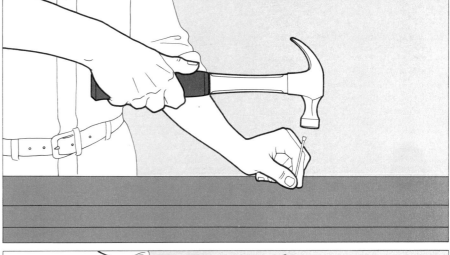

2 **Setting the nail.** Holding a nail punch near its tip between thumb and index finger, centre the recessed tip over the head of the nail. Rest your little finger on the wood to steady your hand, then hit the top of the punch solidly with the hammer to drive the head of the nail about 1 mm below the surface of the wood.

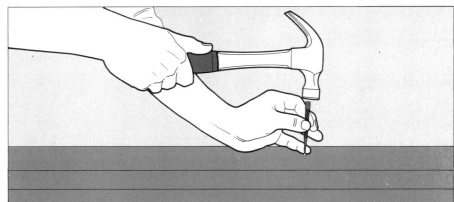

Four Ways to Pull a Nail

Using pincers. To protect the wood surface, position a thin scrap of timber next to the nail. With the pincers, grip the nail as close as possible to the surface of the wood. Rock the pincers slightly on their curved jaws to loosen the nail, then push down on the protected side of the wood and lever the nail out.

If the nail emerges only part way from the wood, release the nail, grip it further down the shank and repeat the technique.

For a nail head that is below the surface of the wood, chisel round the head until the pincer claws can grip it.

Some pincers have a claw on one handle which can be used for removing small tacks *(inset)*.

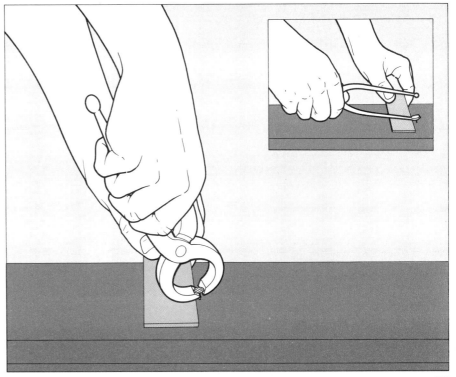

Freeing a nail with a curved claw. Slip the claw of the hammer round the head of the nail and pull the handle of the hammer until the nail head has been drawn a few millimetres above the surface of the wood. Set the head of the hammer against an offcut of wood, re-engage the claw and lever the nail out of the wood.

Using a nail bar. The claw of this nail bar is set round the head of the nail—if the head is below the surface of the wood, strike the curved section at the back of the tool with a rubber-faced mallet to drive the claw under the head. Then pull back on the handle to remove the nail. When working on moulding, set a thin piece of scrap wood under the heel of the nail bar to protect the wood.

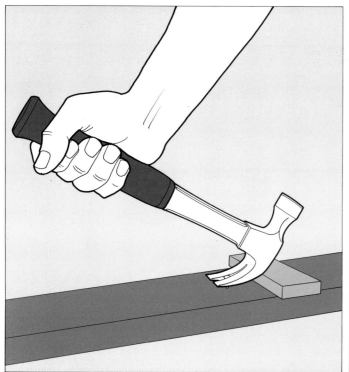

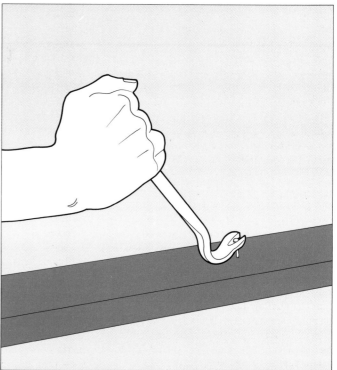

Using a nail puller. This special tool pulls nails quickly and easily. Position the pincers above the nail head, opening them so they are slightly wider than the nail head *(right)*. Hold the handle attached to the pincers, then raise the sliding iron handle and slam it down repeatedly to sink the pincers beneath the nail head. Close the pincers round the head.

Tilt the pincers sideways *(far right)*, using the short handle attached to the pincers as a lever. Slowly pull the nail.

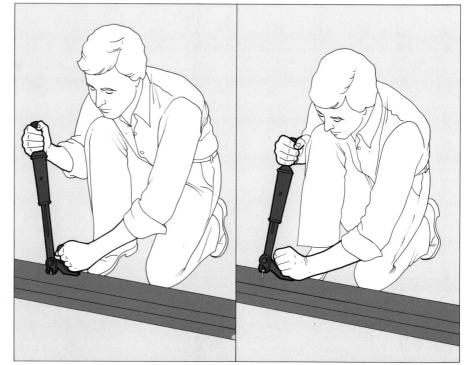

The Extra Strength of a Wood Screw

As fasteners of wood, screws have several advantages over nails. They bind pieces tighter, they do not mar the surface either entering or exiting and, with the proper pilot holes, they do not split wood. But since they take more time and trouble to use than nails, they are reserved for joints that need extra strength or precision assembly or that may have to be dismantled.

The fuss involved in installing screws is minimized by using the right tools—properly maintained—not only to drive the screws but to drill the holes they require. All screws need at least one hole and some need as many as three. A pilot hole is the only hole required for those screws that are threaded all the way to the head, like sheetmetal screws or the screws for plywood.

Other screws require additional holes. Standard wood screws and coach screws have smooth shanks between their threads and their heads; to accommodate the shank, a shallow hole slightly wider than the pilot hole is needed. If the screw head is to be set flush with or below the surface of the wood—a necessity with flat-head screws but optional with other types—a still shallower hole, the diameter of the screw head, is required. A two or three-tier screw hole can be made with regular bits used one after the other, but the special bit called a combination countersink (page 53, bottom) does the entire job in a single step.

A properly drilled hole makes driving a screw easy, if you use a screwdriver of the appropriate type and tip. The tip should also be sharp and it must be the right size so that it fits snugly into the screw head slot. Using the wrong type and the wrong size tip may ruin the slot or damage the tip.

As important as the right size and type is sharpness. Rounded edges or ends will cause the screwdriver tip to slip. When wear rounds away the original sharp, straight forms of the tip, restore the original shape with a grinding wheel. Reserve your good, sharp screwdrivers for driving screws, and keep an old one for such odd jobs as opening paint cans and levering up floorboards.

There are many styles and types of screwdrivers to serve special needs. Some have offset right-angle handles, extra short or extra long shanks, easy-to-grip knob handles, or ratchet drives. A screwdriver bit in a brace is useful for driving in large screws in tight places.

For speed, a spiral-ratchet screwdriver is a useful hand tool. Models range in length from 260 to 700 mm; the appropriate type and size of bit can be fitted to the chuck. A variable-speed electric drill that you have fitted with a screwdriver bit is even faster, but it should be used only where marring the surface of the wood is of no consequence—the bit can chew into the wood if it slips from the screw head. A purpose-made screwdriver drill is the best solution because it stops automatically once the screw is at the set depth.

Using a spiral-ratchet screwdriver. With the ratchet shifter forwards, hold the chuck sleeve between thumb, index and middle fingers as you insert the bit tip into the screw head; push the handle forwards (below, top). When the handle meets the sleeve, pull the handle out and push it forwards in repeated strokes.

When the resistance of the wood makes it difficult to drive the screw this way, disengage the screwdriver, push the handle to the chuck sleeve and turn the locking ring anticlockwise. The screwdriver can now be used like a conventional screwdriver except that its ratchet mechanism can be left in action to ease the job: you can turn your hand and wrist anticlockwise without loosening your grip or removing the bit from the screw.

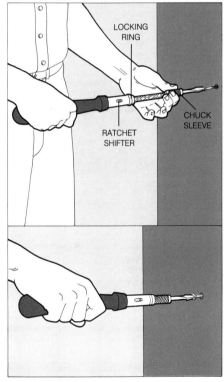

LOCKING RING

RATCHET SHIFTER

CHUCK SLEEVE

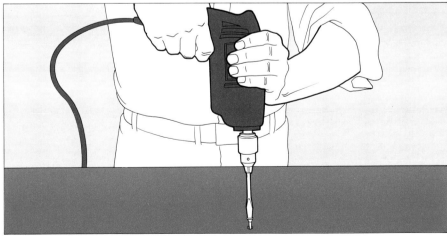

Using an electric drill. With one hand gripping the drill handle, set the palm of the other on top of the motor housing for working vertically, underneath the motor housing for working horizontally, and drive the screw at low speed. Stop the drill as soon as the screw is in place—additional revolutions will strip the threads carved in the wood or break off the screw head.

Finish Joints: Tests of Expert Craftsmanship

The craft of making neat, tightly jointed frames round doors, windows and walls is one of the most demanding tests of woodworking skill. It requires not only mastery of the basic techniques of cutting and shaping wood, but also a repertoire of tricks for fitting and fastening the pieces. Even the most talented professional may fail to achieve a seamless fit at the first try, but must sand, plane, or saw edges—and then seal the gaps with filler for a perfect joint.

The simplest, most common joint is the mitre, which takes moulding round a corner. On door and window architraves, the face of the moulding is cut at an angle for the mitre. On inside corner joints—between the stops of a doorway, perhaps, or between skirting boards that meet at the corner of a room—the ends of boards can be bevelled for a mitre, but a better solution may be a scribed joint, in which the end of one piece (usually the shorter one) is cut to follow the moulded curve of the longer one. Most mitres, whether face cuts or bevels, angle at 45

degrees. However, other angles may be required—for panelling under a staircase, for example, or to fit skirting boards in a window bay.

For some mouldings that meet or end in unusual places, you must work out special solutions. Staircase moulding has to be joined at angles measured to match the slope of the stairs, window mullions must be mated into the shapes of architraving, and ceiling mouldings may need to turn in towards a wall.

In all of these joints, precise marking is crucial. With architraves and interior corners, always nail one piece before you mark the next, so that you will have a bench mark to measure from. Wherever possible, hold short uncut pieces in place to mark length—a more accurate method than using a tape measure; on a mitre cut, mark the longest point of the mitre where the top edge of the moulding meets the back so that you can sight the mark against the mitre-box saw.

Cut mouldings slightly longer than the measurement—1 mm for a short piece of

architraving, as much as 3 mm for a long skirting board—because there is no good remedy for a piece that is too short. Generally, a bit of extra length is absorbed when the piece is nailed and holds the joint tight; if your allowance proves too generous, some can be planed off.

Because pieces of moulding are relatively thin, they warp easily and often have to be straightened as they are nailed. Most warps can be pulled straight by hand and held by nails; bad ones can usually be pulled straight by toenailing.

Moulding presents additional problems. Nails tend to split it, so blunt the points with a hammer or, if needed, drill pilot holes. Furthermore, such costly wood is often given a clear finish to show its grain. This makes it difficult to hide attempts to conceal gaps and nail heads with filler. Precisely fitted joints are essential, and nails should either be punched where tinted filler matches the grain colour or, whenever possible, placed in the moulding recesses so that they are less visible.

Door and Window Architraves

1 **Nailing the top architrave.** Cut the ends of the top architrave at 45 degree angles *(page 28)* and hold the architrave in place over the head lining—set back 6 mm from the inner edge on a door, flush with the edge on most windows. Drive a nail part way through the architrave into the head lining at each lower corner, then nail the upper edge of the architrave into the stud frame at 200 mm intervals. Nail the lower edge of the architrave to the head lining, placing the nails opposite those in the upper edge, then drive home the nails at each end.

If you are nailing the architrave to masonry rather than to a wooden stud, either angle the nails in the upper edge of the architrave back down into the head lining, or else use fine masonry nails to fix the upper edge to the wall.

2 **Fitting the side architrave.** Mark the thin edge of the architrave 1 mm longer than is necessary for an exact fit—it extends from the bottom of the top architrave mitre to the sill of a window or, for a door, to the floor. Square off one end of the stock and mitre the other end outwards, so the thick edge is longer than the thin.

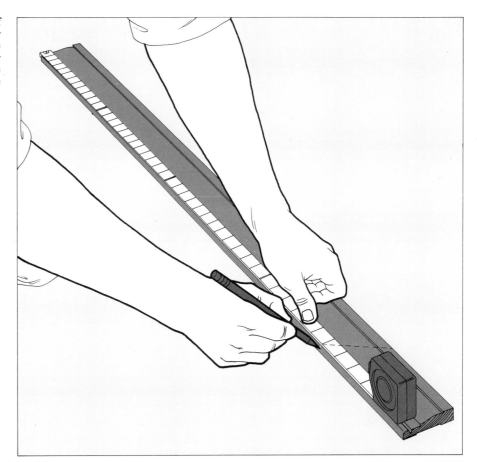

3 **Nailing up the side architrave.** Fit the side architrave as tightly as possible against the top architrave and, at 200 mm intervals, drive nails half way through the side architrave into the studs and the jamb. If the outer edge of the side architrave backs on to masonry, either skew the nails back into the jamb, or use masonry nails. Leave about 6 mm of each of the nails protruding from the architrave.

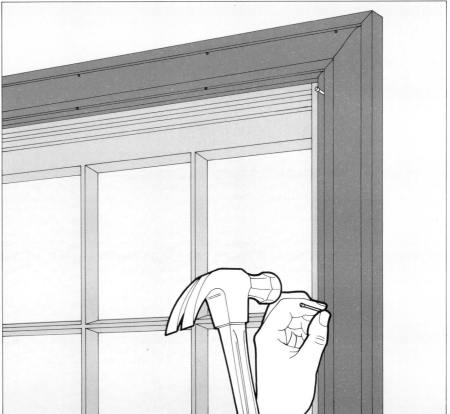

4 Adjusting the architrave. If you find gaps, first try to close them by tapping against the sides with a hammer and wood block. If the joint remains ragged, with edges meeting at only a few points, cut along the joint line with a small tenon saw called a bead saw, then tap the architrave again to close the gaps.

5 Lock-nailing the joint. To keep the joint firmly fastened and prevent its opening when the wood shrinks, hold the side architrave in place and drive a 37 mm oval nail straight down through the top architrave into the side architrave.

Then hold the top architrave and drive a nail horizontally into it through the side architrave. Use a nail punch to sink these nails and then drive and sink the remaining nails in the side architrave. Cover all nail heads with filler.

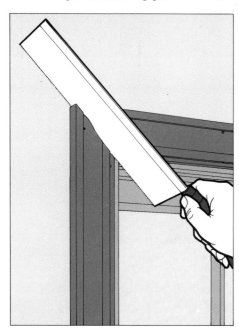

Scribing a Joint

1 Marking for a scribed joint. Butt a piece of skirting board into the corner and nail it to the wall. Mitre the end of a second piece at 45 degrees, angling the cut inwards from the back of the piece to the front so that the cut creates a profile of the skirting board along the line of the cut; then mark along the curved profile line with the side of a pencil to make the profile more visible.

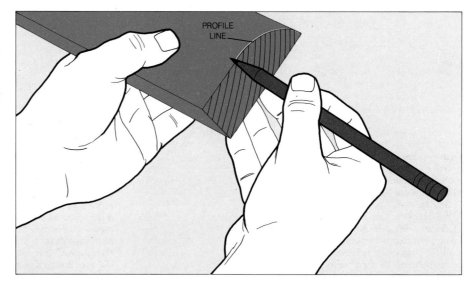

PROFILE LINE

2 Making the cut. With a coping saw aligned at a right angle to the face of the skirting board, cut along the profile line. The scribed moulding should now fit against the face of the skirting board you have installed at the corner *(inset)*.

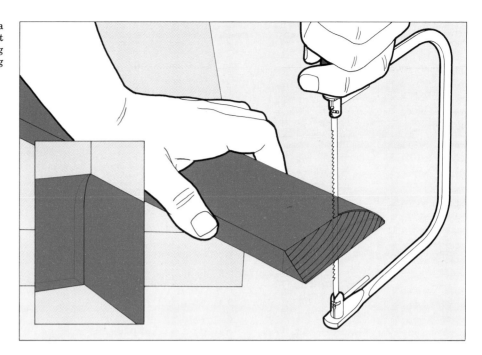

Fitting a Corner—and Fixing a Bad Fit

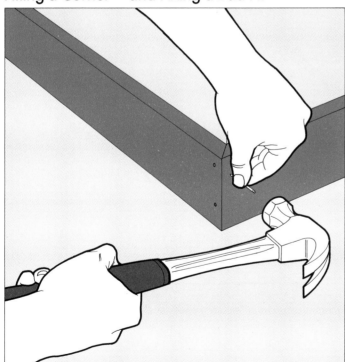

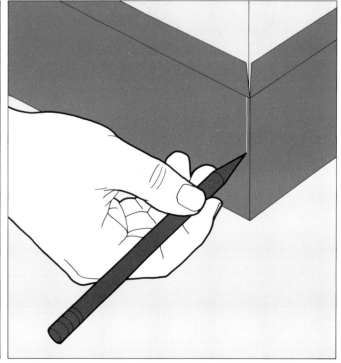

Fastening the skirting board. Mitre two pieces of skirting at 45 degrees and hold them in place against the outside corner. If the joint is tight—this will occur only if the walls meet in a true right angle—nail the skirting board to the wall. Use 60 mm oval or lost-head nails if fixing to studs or wall pads; use 60 mm masonry nails or 75 mm cut clasps on plastered blockwork. Lock-nail the mitres by driving in two 37 mm oval nails horizontally from each side. If the joint gaps, remedy it as described right or overleaf.

Closing a gap at the back of the joint. If the wall angle is greater than 90 degrees and forces the joint open at the back, hold the skirting boards in place and measure the gap between the backs of the two pieces. If the gap is less than 6 mm, mark a line on one piece of skirting board at the measured distance from the corner; if the gap is more than 6 mm, mark half the measurement on each piece of skirting. Use a block plane to shave the wood to the line or lines *(page 76)*.

A gap at the front. If the wall angle is less than 90 degrees and forces the joint open at the front, use a trimming knife to shave away wood—not more than 3 mm at a time—from the inner edge of sections up to 100 mm wide; for larger sections, use a coping saw but make the cuts in the same way. Start just below the top of the skirting—do not shave the top, which will squeeze to a tight fit—and work down to the bottom. To correct a large gap, shave wood from both sides of the joint.

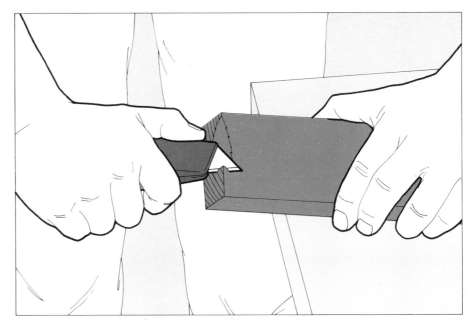

Trimming the Angles of a Staircase

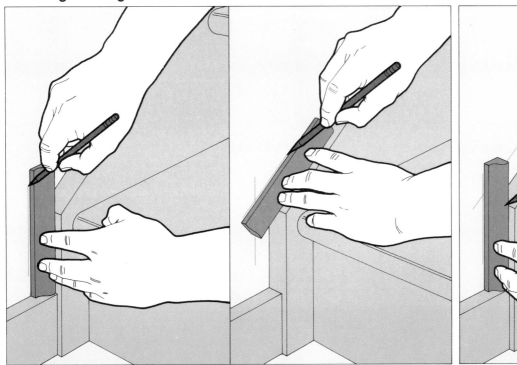

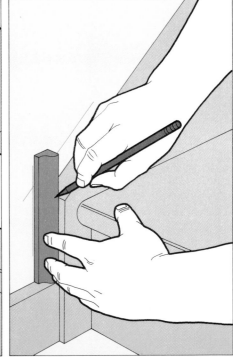

1 Marking the wall. Place the bottom of a piece of moulding along one side of the angle and use the top as a straightedge to draw a line on the wall *(above, left)*. Move the moulding to the other side of the angle and use it to draw a second line on the wall, intersecting the first *(above, right)*.

2 Marking the moulding. Hold a piece of moulding in position at the first side of the angle; mark the top edge of the moulding at the intersection of the drawn lines on the wall, and the bottom edge at the point of the angle. Repeat the procedure with a second piece of moulding held at the other side of the angle.

Set a mitre box to cut each piece along a line between the marks you have made; the mitre cuts will fit the mouldings to the angle.

Splices and End Pieces

A mitre-lap joint. Try to avoid splicing two pieces of identical skirting along a single wall, but if you must make a joint on a very long wall, do so at a stud or wall pad, mitring the ends of two pieces at 45 degrees in the same direction. That is, set the mitre-box saw in the same position for both left and right pieces. Lap the cuts at a stud or pad and drive two 60 mm lost-head or oval nails through the splice into the stud or pad.

If working on blockwork or bricks without pads, use 60 mm masonry nails or 75 mm cut clasps to fix the spliced ends.

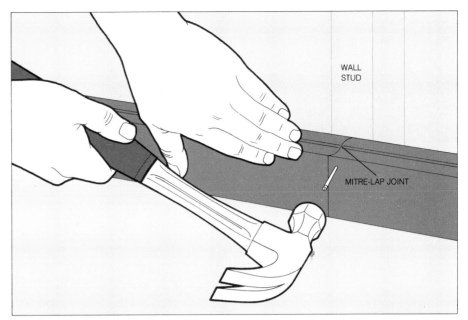

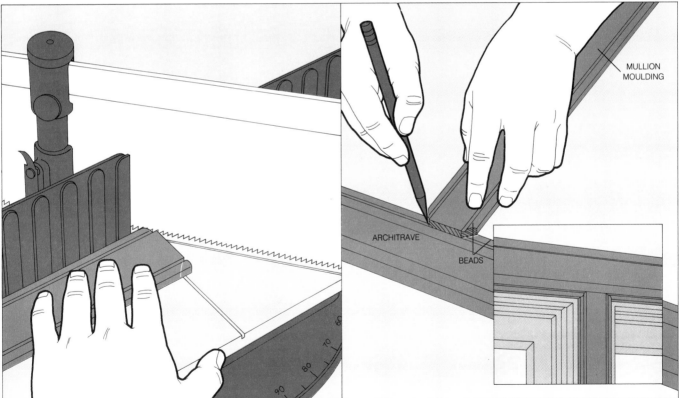

Splicing at right angles. To trim a horizontal transom or vertical mullion in a door or window unit containing two or more sections, you must fit special transom or mullion moulding at right angles to the top or side architraves. For most beaded architraves, use moulding like that illustrated—a flat centre section and edge beads the same thickness as the architrave beads. Mitre only the beads on each side, as indicated by the cutting line *(above, left)*. Place the mitred end of the moulding over the bead of the architrave and draw lines on the architrave along each mitre cut *(above, right)*. Using a coping saw, cut out the section of architrave between the lines so that the end of the moulding fits tightly into the body of the architrave, with the beads of the moulding and architrave forming neat mitre joints *(inset)*.

If you cannot match beaded moulding for the technique described, use transom or mullion moulding that is thinner than the edge thickness of the architrave. Do not mitre it or cut into the architrave; cut the moulding square to butt under the architrave edge. If you use unbeaded architraves—such as the smoothly curved "pencil-round" type—cut a matching moulding for a transom or mullion to a 45 degree point, and trace and cut a mating notch into the architrave.

A mitred return. To end a run of moulding that does not join another—sometimes necessary for chair rails and ceiling mouldings—mark the end point on the face and mitre the piece in towards the back. Mitre the end of a second piece in the opposite direction, from the back in towards the face, and cut it at a 90 degree angle at the point where the mitre cut meets the back, creating a triangular wedge *(inset)*. Glue the wedge to the mitred end of the first piece of moulding, then nail it in place with 25 or 45 mm panel pins.

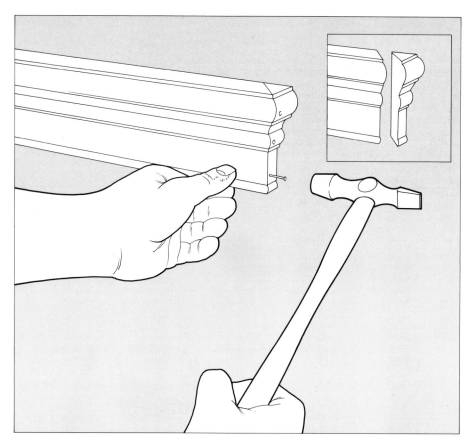

A Plinth for an Awkward Corner

A plinth block. Where different mouldings meet at floor level—in this typical example, a traditional door moulding and a more severely styled skirting board—cut a rectangular "plinth" block from an offcut of wood. Make it slightly wider, higher and thicker than the mouldings and fit it to the mouldings with butt joints. When you add a cover moulding, mitre its end to meet the outer edge of the block. A plinth block that is more than 75 mm wide can be nailed in place like a short piece of skirting board; smaller ones should be glued to the wall and to the moulding ends.

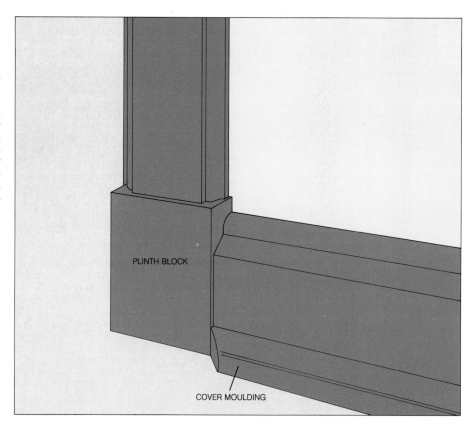

PLINTH BLOCK

COVER MOULDING

A Tricky Mitre Cut for a Cornice Moulding

An interior corner. To make a mitre joint *(inset)*, measure from corner to corner, mark the distance on the bottom edge of a length of ceiling moulding and place the moulding upside down in a mitre box, with the bottom of the moulding tight against the fence. Place the piece you want to cut on the opposite side of the saw blade from its position on the ceiling—that is, to the right side of the blade for the left-hand corner piece, and vice versa. Set the saw for a 45 degree cut to the right to cut the left-hand piece, as illustrated in this example; set the handle to the left for a right-hand piece. For a neater but somewhat more difficult alternative, scribe a corner piece as you would a skirting board *(pages 108–109)*.

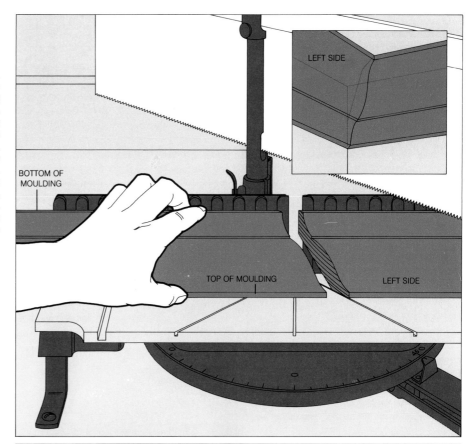

An exterior joint. For an exterior corner *(inset)*, which cannot be scribed and must be mitred, place the ceiling moulding upside down and reversed in the mitre box as you would for an interior joint, but do not reverse the saw's direction. Thus, cut the piece for the left side of the corner with the saw handle at the left, and the piece for the right side with the handle at the right.

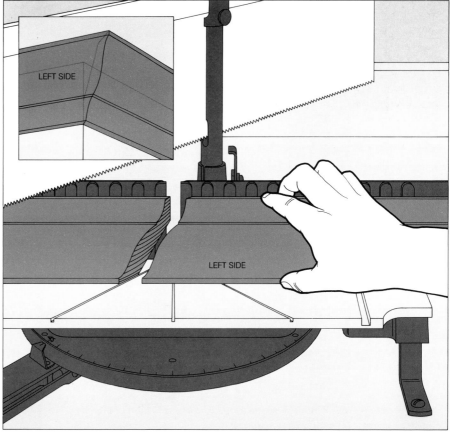

Intricacies of Traditional Carpenter's Joints

In many areas of a modern home, simple nailing does not suffice and traditional woodworking joints are still necessary. Much stronger connections can be formed with mortise and tenon, housing, tongue and groove, and rebate joints. These joints are used in floors, staircases, doorframes and window frames, where strength is critical; in roof soffits and exterior cladding, where a weathertight seal is needed; and in interior panelling, for neat appearance.

The way two boards meet determines the type of joint used. Where boards meet at right angles—either end to end, as with the side and head linings of a door, or edge to edge, as with a staircase tread and riser—one of two joints is used. The stronger is the housing joint in which the square end of one board fits into a housing groove near the end of the other. In the slightly weaker rebate joint, the square end fits into a rebate step at the end of the other board.

Where the boards meet edge to edge, the housings and rebates can be combined in a joint commonly found in stairway construction. The housings or rebates for these joints usually have to be cut on the job with a router or radial arm saw, using the techniques shown in Chapter 3, but if a number of identical joints are used, the boards can be cut by a timber merchant.

For those boards that meet edge to edge on a flat surface—hardwood floorboards, plywood subflooring, interior wall panelling, exterior cladding and roof decks—the joints must combine a neat appearance with flexibility, so that the wood can contract and expand slightly as moisture and temperature change. On interior panelling and exterior cladding, a variation on the rebate joint is often used: boards are machined with a rebate along the face of one edge and a matching rebate along the back of the other, so that the two overlap when the panelling is installed.

Panelling, cladding and flooring can also be fitted together with tongue and groove joints: each board has a groove machined along the centre of one edge and a matching tongue (made by cutting rebates on each side) on the other. The tongue is generally a fraction shallower than the groove, which ensures that the board faces fit tightly together.

Because flat joints on walls and floors involve a series of boards, they require careful planning and alignment. When the boards are applied vertically on a timber-frame wall, rows of 100 by 50 mm noggings must be nailed horizontally between the studs, one-quarter, one-half and three-quarters of the way up the wall. On a masonry wall, 50 by 20 mm battens spaced 400 mm apart must be fixed to the wall with masonry nails; position the battens horizontally for panelling and vertically for cladding. To make sure a thin, unsightly board is not left at the end of the job, the width of the boards being used (plus any gap) should be divided into the length of the wall or floor. If the amount left over is less than 50 mm, both the first and last boards should be trimmed equally so that both are more than 50 mm wide.

Where the joint between a board and a wall will be exposed, the board may need to be scribed and sawn or planed to the irregular contour of the wall; and in hardwood panelling, pilot holes must be drilled to prevent the nails splitting the wood.

The third type of joint, the mortise and tenon (pages 118–123), is used when two boards meet, face up, at right angles, as in a window sash or panelled door. The projecting tenon at the end of one board fits into the mortise hole in the other board and is secured by glue or dowels. Mortise and tenon joints are less common in new window sashes and doors because modern glues and machine woodworking have supplanted them to some extent, but they may be needed in repairing old woodwork.

Three Basic Right-Angle Joints

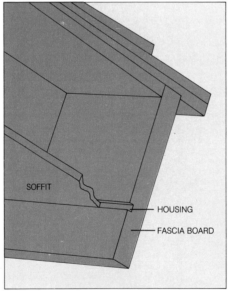

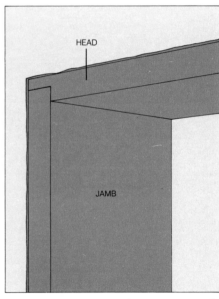

A housing joint. Under the eave of this house roof, the edge of the plywood soffit fits into a housing in the back of the fascia board, forming a strong, weathertight joint. The housing—its depth usually one-third to one-half the thickness of the fascia board—prevents the soffit from moving up or down; the joint could work loose only if the soffit and fascia board pulled apart. Housing joints also fit the top edge of stair risers to the undersides of treads. The same joint can be used between the ends of boards: the head linings of doors in internal partition walls sometimes fit into housings in the side linings.

A rebate joint. At the top of this door lining, the jamb fits into a step, or rebate, in the head. Rebate joints like this are also used for window and trap-door linings. The same joint can be used between the edges of boards: the back edge of a stair tread may fit into a rebate at the bottom of the riser above it, for example.

Rebate joints are somewhat weaker than housing joints, because nails alone are not as strong as the combination of a housed groove and nails; however, because a rebate joint forms a square corner, it can fit into a right-angled frame, and a housing joint cannot.

A rebate and housing joint. On this staircase, the back of each tread is rebated to fit into a housing near the bottom of each riser. The resulting rebate and housing joint combines the best of both types: it is nearly as strong as a housing, but can be made at the edge of a board like a rebate. In such a staircase, the tops of the risers and the fronts of the treads are often joined in the same way, but as a matter of convenience only; a housing would work just as well there.

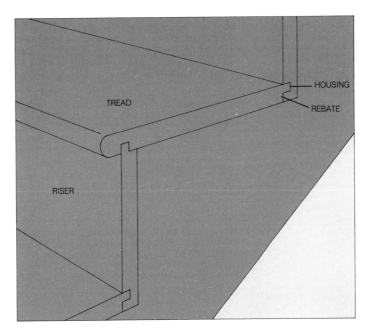

Flexible Joints for Walls and Floors

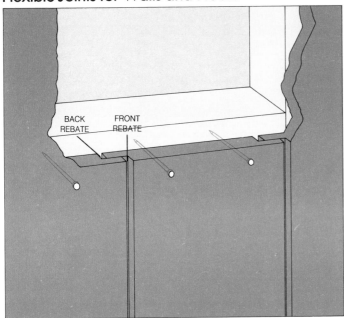

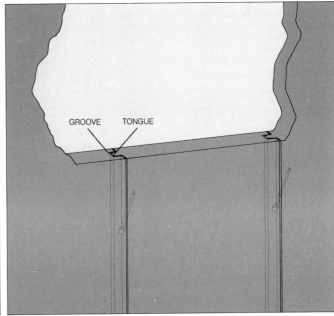

Rebate joints. In this interior-wall panelling, each board has a rebate along one edge of the exposed face and another along the opposite edge at the back. The projection at the face overlaps the back rebate to conceal cracks; there is a gap—called a reveal—between each projection and the body of the next board, to allow boards to expand and contract without buckling or splitting. The same joint can be used for horizontal panelling or, without the gaps between boards, for weathertight exterior cladding.

Tongue and groove joints. In this panelling, each board has a groove along the centre of one edge and a matching tongue along the other. Tongues and grooves interlock in nearly invisible joints and the boards are fastened with "secret nails", which are driven at an angle through the tongue of each board so that they are hidden by the groove of the next board. Tongue and groove joints are stronger and more flexible than rebate joints. They are used for wood flooring, because they resist squeaking and warping; for plywood subflooring, because they eliminate the need for rows of blocking to support the edges of the sheets; and for exterior cladding, because they resist air infiltration.

Assembling a Right-Angle Joint

A housing joint. Slip the end of one board into a housing on a second board (in this example the first board is the head lining of a doorframe, the second is a side lining), then drive pairs of nails in V patterns through the housing, from the second board into the first *(inset)*. The opposing angles of the nails help keep the joint tight.

If the first board is more than 12 mm thick and so warped that it will not slip easily into the housing, plane the end of the board down; forcing such a board into place can cause it to split.

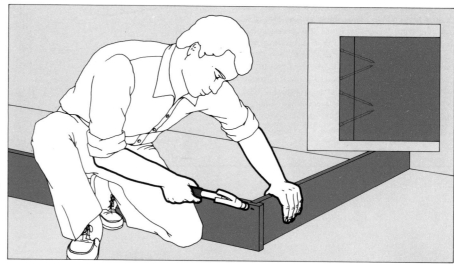

A rebate joint. For a joint commonly used to fasten door and window linings, fit and nail the end of one board into a rebate in a second board. Near the edges of the rebated board, drive a pair of nails in a V pattern through the rebate into the end of the unrebated board, angling the nails towards the middle of the board; brace the other end against a wall to keep the joint tight while you nail. Then drive a second pair of nails through the unrebated board into the end of the rebated one *(right)*, starting the nails near the middle of the board and angling them out towards the edges.

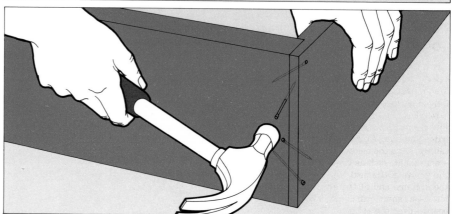

Installing a Set of Rebated Panels

1 **Aligning the first boards.** Prepare a timber-frame wall by installing noggings between the studs; on masonry walls, attach a series of horizontal battens *(page 114)*. At the right-hand side of the wall, nail a plumb starter board to the top and sole plates and to the noggings or battens. If you are also panelling the adjacent wall, rebate both edges of the starter—a normal 25 mm rebate on the left edge, and on the right, a rebate equal to the thickness of a board and the width of the planned gap between boards. If you are panelling only one side of a room, do not rebate the right edge; instead, fit it to the adjacent wall.

Set a 5 mm plywood spacer into the left-hand rebate of the starter board near the top of the wall, slide the edge of the next board against the spacer and drive two 32 mm panel pins through the face of the new board—not through the rebates—into the top plate. Place the spacer into the rebate near the bottom of the board and nail the board to the bottom plate; then nail the board to each of the noggings. Repeat this procedure for each of the succeeding four boards.

2 Keeping the boards vertical. Every six boards, fasten the top of a board with only one nail, then hold a level in the rebate near the bottom of the board. Swing the board from side to side until it is plumb, then nail the board in the normal way.

At the left end of the wall, install the starter board of the adjacent wall *(Step 1)* if you plan to put panelling on the other side of the corner. Scribe and cut the last board so that it will fit snugly into the rebate of the starter board (or against the wall, if you are not panelling the adjacent wall), then nail it in place.

Fitting and Nailing Tongue and Groove Joints

1 Driving the boards together. On a wall, align the first board against an adjacent wall, with the tongue facing out; plumb it with a level and nail through its face into the top and sole plates and into noggings or battens like those used for rebated panelling *(opposite, bottom)*. On a floor or ceiling, align the board by measuring from a reference point, such as the bottom of a wall. Slide the groove of the next board on to the tongue of the first one and fit the groove of a hammering block—a short offcut of tongue and groove board—over the tongue of the new board near one end. Strike the block firmly with a mallet, driving the new board on to the tongue of the previous one; slide the block along the board as you work so that the board seats evenly.

2 Nailing the tongue. Drive nails at a 45 degree angle part way through the base of the tongue, where it meets the body of the board, into the noggings or battens behind the board; sink the nails with a nail punch, taking care not to splinter the tongue. If a board is more than 200 mm wide, face-nail it through the middle; narrower boards need not be face-nailed.

On a vertical surface, plumb every sixth board as you would a rebated one *(Step 2, above)* and adjust it by driving one end tight with the hammering block; on a horizontal surface, measure from the edge of the board to the reference point. At the end of the wall or floor, cut off the tongue edge of the next-to-last board and install it by nailing through its face. Scribe the last board on the tongue edge to match it to the wall *(page 35, bottom)*, cut it along the scribed line and face-nail it, with the groove against the cut edge of the next-to-last board.

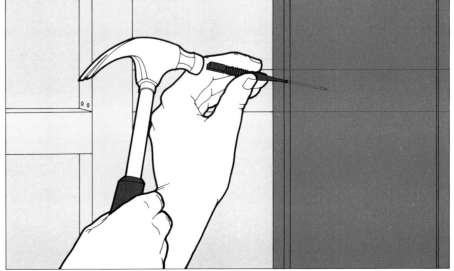

Setting a Tenon into a Mortise

In a mortise and tenon joint, the projecting tenon of one piece fits so snugly into the rectangular mortise hole of the other that they are joined together almost as strongly as if they were a single piece of wood. Such strength is particularly important in window sashes and panelled doors, which are subjected to repeated stresses that would quickly pull apart a simple butt joint.

The tenon is always made on the shorter of the two pieces—generally the horizontal rail of a door or window. This is done so that the short piece can be clamped vertically in a vice when it is sawn and chiselled as a long piece could not be. If you are making several joints for a complete frame, glue and clamp all the joints at the same time *(page 121)*.

To make a strong, precise joint, you will need a special tool called a mortising gauge, which has two sharp points that can be set to mark both sides of a mortise at once and to transfer the marks to the tenon without changing the adjustment.

Modern mortise and tenon joints are generally fastened by glue alone, but the old-fashioned technique of using a cross-wise dowel to pin such a joint together still has its uses. To mend a joint that has popped loose, you can sometimes drive the pieces back together, drill a hole through the joint and glue in a dowel; the alternative method—dismantling the joint, then cleaning and regluing it—is difficult and time-consuming.

A through mortise and tenon joint. The tenon is one-third the thickness of the tenon piece and its length is equivalent to the full width of the mortise piece. The sides of the tenon, which fit snugly into the mortise, provide the maximum possible surface area for gluing; this reinforces the strength of the joint. The shoulders of the mortise and of the tenon, on the bodies of the boards, fit together flush on all sides.

A through mortise and tenon joint is typically used to join the intermediate horizontal rails of a panelled door to the sides, for securing transoms and mullions in window frames and for fixing banisters in stair handrails.

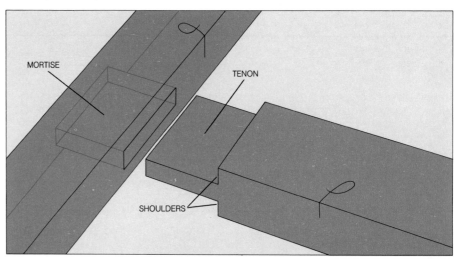

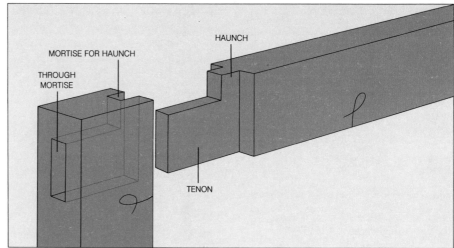

A haunched mortise and tenon joint. In this joint, which is typically used at the corners between the top and bottom rails of a panelled door and the sides, the width of both the tenon and the through mortise is reduced by one-third. When the edge strip of the full-width tenon is sawn off, however, a small piece—the "haunch"—is left at the shoulders to prevent the tenon from twisting out of alignment with the mortise piece. An extension of the through mortise is chiselled out to accept the tenon haunch. The tenon is held in position by the end of the mortise piece, and cannot slip out upwards or downwards.

Assembling a Through Mortise and Tenon Joint

1 Setting the mortising gauge. Choose a mortise chisel whose width is approximately one-third the thickness of the wood to be joined; rest the chisel on a workbench, the tip overhanging the edge of the bench. Loosen the thumbscrew on top of the gauge fence, hold the gauge to the chisel tip and set the gauge points to the chisel-tip width by turning the adjusting thumbscrew at the end of the bar. Hold the gauge against the edge of the board to be mortised, slide the bar through the fence until the points are centred on the board and tighten the fence thumbscrew.

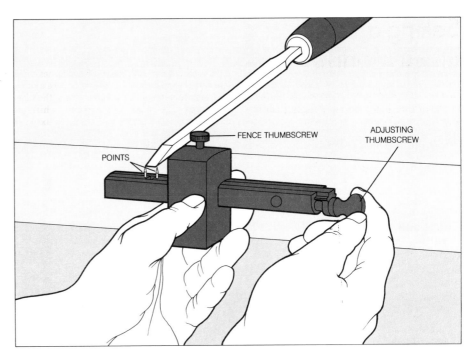

POINTS

FENCE THUMBSCREW

ADJUSTING THUMBSCREW

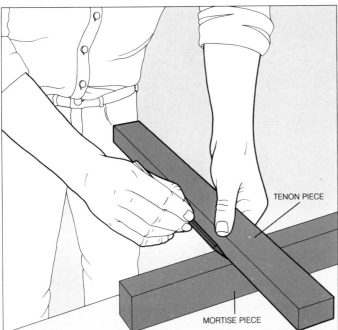

TENON PIECE

MORTISE PIECE

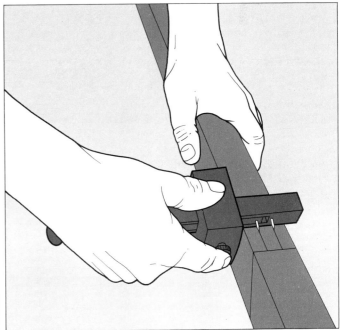

2 Marking the mortise width. Choose the better looking side of both mortise and tenon pieces, and on each piece mark this face side and an adjoining edge with a pencil line. Whenever the tenon piece is brought into contact with the mortise piece, ensure that the face sides are matching.

To mark the width of the mortise, hold the tenon piece against the marked edge of the mortise piece and draw pencil lines along the latter's edges *(above)*. Use a combination square to continue these lines round to the opposite edge of the mortise piece.

3 Using the mortising gauge. To mark the thickness of the mortise, hold the gauge against one face and score lines with the points *(above)*. Check that the lines are centred by holding the gauge against the opposite face and again scoring lines; if the two sets of lines do not coincide, loosen the thumbscrew and adjust the gauge. Repeat this procedure to mark the mortise thickness on the opposite edge of the mortise piece.

Secure the mortise piece in a vice or cramp with one edge facing up. Using a mortise chisel and mallet, and following the instructions on page 64, chisel out the mortise to about half way through the wood. Then release the mortise piece from the vice, turn it over and chisel out the rest of the mortise from the other side.

4 **Marking the tenon.** Mark the length of the tenon from the width of the mortise piece, and use a combination square to continue the lines round all four sides of the wood. Keeping the gauge at the same setting that was used for the mortise, mark out the tenon thickness along both sides and the top edge *(right)*. To sharpen the lines marking the tenon shoulders, score over the pencil lines with a trimming knife.

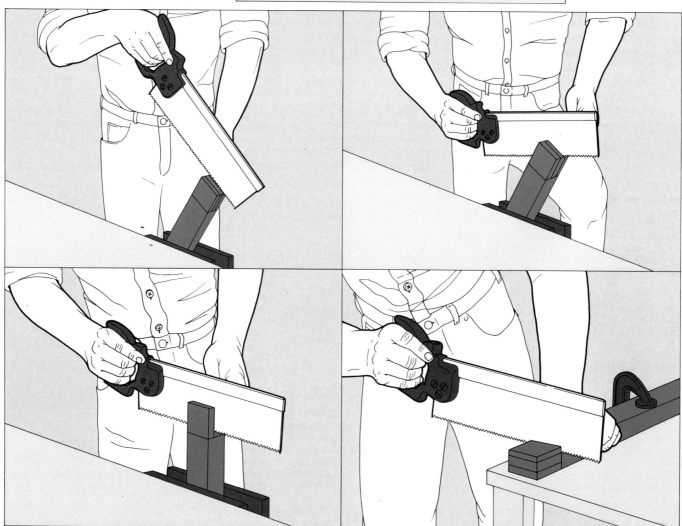

5 **Sawing the tenon.** Secure the tenon piece at an angle of 45 degrees in a woodworking vice, and begin to saw along the waste side of one of the scored lines on the top edge *(top, left)*. When the kerf is established, gradually lower the angle of the saw and cut down the side score line to the shoulder *(top, right)*. Release the wood from the vice, turn it round, secure it again at a 45 degree angle and saw down the opposite score line. Then, with the wood secured upright, saw straight across to the bottom of the tenon *(above, left)*. Release the wood from the vice and clamp it horizontally; saw off the waste wood along the shoulder line *(above, right)*. Repeat the above procedure to saw off the opposite side of the tenon. Finally, to ease the fitting of the tenon into the mortise, chamfer the edges of the tenon with a sharp chisel.

6 Test-fitting the joint. Clamp the mortised board horizontally in a vice and push the tenon into the mortise, tapping it gently with a mallet if necessary. Check that the face sides are matching. If you meet strong resistance, pull the tenon out and look for shiny spots on its cheeks—signs of bulges in the mortise or tenon. Use a chisel to pare away the shiny spots, working across the grain with the bevel facing up, then test the joint again. Pare the tenon until you can force it into the mortise, then separate the pieces.

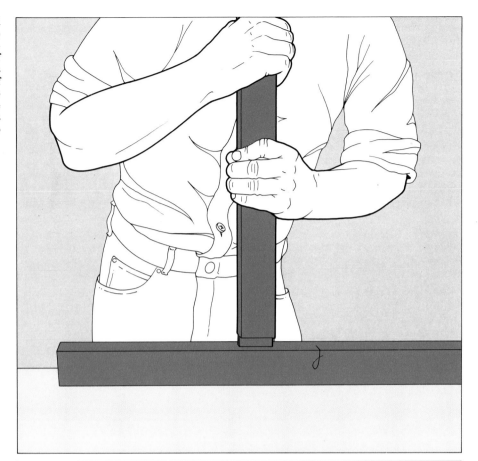

7 Assembling the joint. Spread PVA glue on the tenon with a brush and inside the mortise with a thin scrap of wood; to prevent excess glue from being squeezed out when the joint is assembled, use only enough glue to barely cloud the surface of the wood and do not glue the base of the tenon near the shoulders. Slide the tenon into the mortise (if you are making a window sash or door with several joints, glue and assemble them all at once) and set the pieces flat on a workbench.

Hold the boards together with a long sash cramp, using scrap blocks of wood to protect the surface; pinch the mortise round the cheeks of the tenon with a G-cramp. Check that the joints are perpendicular with a combination square, then tighten the cramps.

Assembling a Haunched Mortise and Tenon Joint

1 Marking the mortise. Using the tenon piece, mark out the full width of the mortise about 25 mm from the end of the mortise piece—this waste piece of wood, known as the horn, will both provide leverage for clamping and prevent the wood from splitting, and will be sawn off when the joint is finished. Mark the thickness of the mortise with a mortising gauge *(page 119, Step 3)*; then, on the side of the mortise piece facing the tenon, mark off the width of the haunch from the top end of the mortise. The haunch width should be one-third of the full mortise width.

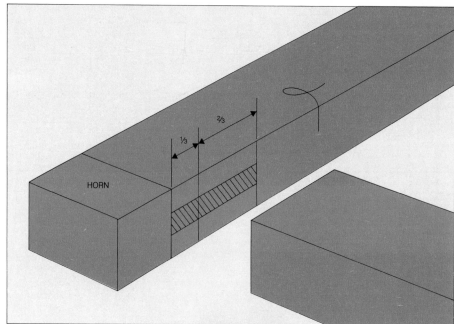

2 Chopping the mortise. Secure the mortise piece with a cramp and chop out the through mortise with a chisel and mallet *(page 119, Step 3)*. Then chop out the mortise for the tenon haunch to a depth equivalent to the width of the tenon *(right)*. Clean out the shavings. Mark and saw the tenon as you would for a full-width through mortise *(page 120)*.

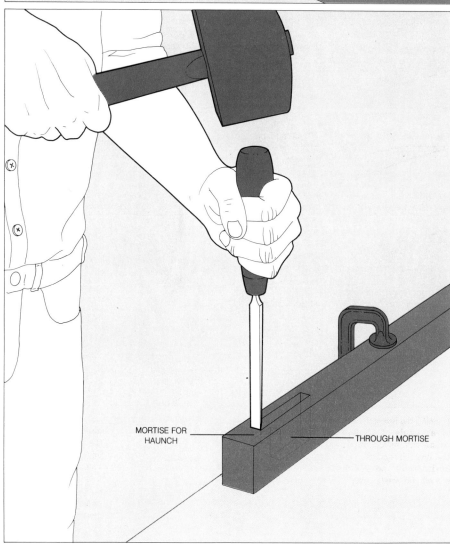

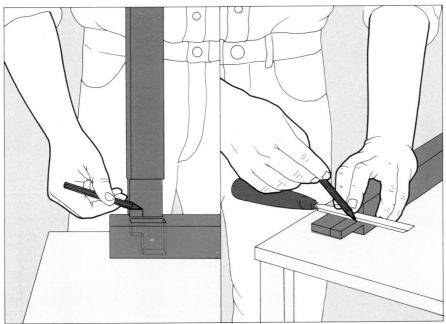

3 **Marking the haunch.** Set the tenon against the mortise and mark the width of the haunch *(far left)*. To mark the depth of the haunch, butt one side of the mortise chisel against the shoulder of the tenon and mark along the other side with a pencil *(left)*.

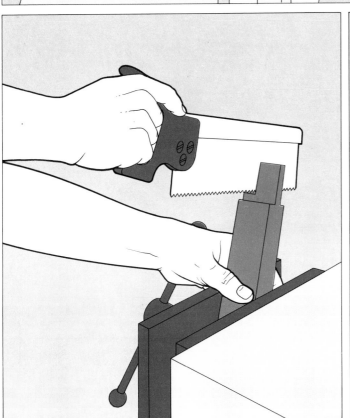

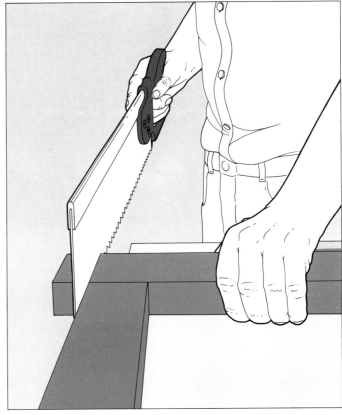

4 **Forming the haunch.** Set the tenon piece in a vice at an angle of 45 degrees and saw down the waste side of the mark indicating the width of the haunch *(above)*. Then clamp the tenon piece horizontally and saw down the second mark to cut off the waste area and form the haunch.

5 **Completing the joint.** Test-fit the tenon in the mortise. If the tenon sticks, pare off wood from the tenon or haunch as necessary with a chisel. For the final fitting, brush PVA glue on the tenon and inside the mortise, assemble the joint and check that it is perpendicular. Clamp the joint with a sash cramp until the glue has completely dried. Saw off the horn *(above)*. Plane as necessary to make all the edges flush.

Picture Credits

The sources for the illustrations in this book are shown below. Credits for the illustrations from left to right are separated by semicolons, from top to bottom by dashes.

Cover: Fil Hunter. 6: Stephen R. Brown. 9, 10: Drawings by Frederic F. Bigio from B-C Graphics. 12–19: Drawings by Frederic F. Bigio from B-C Graphics. 20–25: Drawings by Ray Skibinski. 26–29: Drawings by Eduino Pereira. 30: Drawings by Adsai Hemintranont. 31–32: Drawings by Frederic F. Bigio from B-C Graphics. 33: Drawing by Oxford Illustrators Ltd.— Drawing by Frederic F. Bigio from B-C Graphics. 34–39: Drawings by Walter Hilmers Jr. 40–41: Drawings by John Massey. 42–44: Drawings by Frederic F. Bigio from B-C Graphics. 45: Drawings by Oxford Illustrators Ltd. 46: Drawings (including insert) by John Massey—Drawing by Oxford Illustrators Ltd. 47: Drawing by John Massey—Drawing by Oxford Illustrators Ltd. 48–49: Drawings by Oxford Illustrators Ltd. 50: Stephen R. Brown. 52: Drawing by Walter Hilmers Jr. 53: Drawing by Oxford Illustrators Ltd.—Drawings by Walter Hilmers Jr. 54–56: Drawings by Walter Hilmers Jr. 57: Drawing by Oxford Illustrators Ltd.—Drawings by Walter Hilmers Jr. 58–59: Drawings by Walter Hilmers Jr. 60: Drawing by Whitman Studio, Inc.; Drawing by Oxford Illustrators Ltd. 61: Drawings by Oxford Illustrators Ltd.—Drawing by Whitman Studio Inc. 62: Drawing by Whitman Studio Inc.—Drawing by Whitman Studio Inc.; Drawing by Oxford Illustrators Ltd. 63: Drawing by Oxford Illustrators Ltd.— Drawings by Whitman Studio, Inc. 64: Drawings by Whitman Studio Inc. 65: Drawing by Oxford Illustrators Ltd.— Drawing by Whitman Studio Inc. 66: Drawing by Oxford Illustrators Ltd. 67–69: Drawings by Forte, Inc. 70: Stephen R. Brown. 72–77: Drawings by Peter McGinn. 78–81: Drawings by Walter Hilmers Jr. 82–83: Drawings by John Massey. 84–87: Drawings by Gerry Gallagher. 88–89: Drawings by James Robert Long. 90–95: Drawings by John Massey. 96: Martin Brigdale. 98: Drawing by Oxford Illustrators Ltd. 99: Drawings by Oxford Illustrators Ltd.; Drawings by Frederic F. Bigio from B-C Graphics. 100: Drawing by Oxford Illustrators Ltd. 101–102: Drawings by Frederic F. Bigio from B-C Graphics. 103: Drawings by Frederic F. Bigio from B-C Graphics (2)—Drawings by Oxford Illustrators Ltd. (2). 104–105: Drawings by Frederic F. Bigio from B-C Graphics. 106–115: Drawings by John Massey. 116–118: Drawings by Walter Hilmers Jr. 119: Drawing by Walter Hilmers Jr.—Drawings by Oxford Illustrators Ltd. 120–123: Drawings by Oxford Illustrators Ltd.

Acknowledgements

The editors would like to thank the following: Black and Decker Power Tools, Maidenhead, Berks.; GKN Fasteners, Wednesbury, West Midlands; Aquila Kegan, London; The Miller, Morris and Brooker Group, Slough, Berks.; Timber Research and Development Association, High Wycombe, Bucks.; Woodworking Machinery Suppliers Association, London.

Index/Glossary

Included in this index are definitions of some of the technical terms used in this book. Page references in italics indicate an illustration of the subject mentioned.

Metric Conversion Chart

Approximate equivalents—length

Millimetres to inches		Inches to millimetres	
1	1/32	1/32	1
2	1/16	1/16	2
3	1/8	1/8	3
4	5/32	3/16	5
5	3/16	1/4	6
6	1/4	5/16	8
7	9/32	3/8	10
8	5/16	7/16	11
9	11/32	1/2	13
10 (1cm)	3/8	9/16	14
11	7/16	5/8	16
12	15/32	11/16	17
13	1/2	3/4	19
14	9/16	13/16	21
15	19/32	7/8	22
16	5/8	15/16	24
17	11/16	1	25
18	23/32	2	51
19	3/4	3	76
20	25/32	4	102
25	1	5	127
30	1 3/16	6	152
40	1 9/16	7	178
50	1 15/16	8	203
60	2 3/8	9	229
70	2 3/4	10	254
80	3 1/8	11	279
90	3 9/16	12 (1ft)	305
100	3 15/16	13	330
200	7 7/8	14	356
300	11 13/16	15	381
400	15 3/4	16	406
500	19 11/16	17	432
600	23 3/8	18	457
700	27 9/16	19	483
800	31 1/2	20	508
900	35 7/16	24 (2ft)	610
1000 (1m)	39 3/8		

Metres to feet/inches

2	6' 7"
3	9' 10"
4	13' 1"
5	16' 5"
6	19' 8"
7	23' 0"
8	26' 3"
9	29' 6"
10	32' 10"
20	65' 7"
50	164' 0"
100	328' 7"

Yards to metres

1	0.914
2	1.83
3	2.74
4	3.65
5	4.57
6	5.49
7	6.40
8	7.32
9	8.23
10	9.14
20	18.29
50	45.72
100	91.44

Conversion factors

Length

1 millimetre (mm)	= 0.0394 in
1 centimetre (cm)/10 mm	= 0.3937 in
1 metre/100 cm	= 39.37 in/3.281 ft/1.094 yd
1 kilometre (km)/1000 metres	= 1093.6 yd/0.6214 mile
1 inch (in)	= 25.4 mm/2.54 cm
1 foot (ft)/12 in	= 304.8 mm/30.48 cm/0.3048 metre
1 yard (yd)/3 ft	= 914.4 mm/91.44 cm/0.9144 metre
1 mile/1760 yd	= 1609.344 metres/1.609 km

Area

1 square centimetre (sq cm)/ 100 square millimetres (sq mm)	= 0.155 sq in
1 square metre (sq metre)/10,000 sq cm	= 10.764 sq ft/1.196 sq yd
1 are/100 sq metres	= 119.60 sq yd/0.0247 acre
1 hectare (ha)/100 ares	= 2.471 acres/0.00386 sq mile
1 square inch (sq in)	= 645.16 sq mm/6.4516 sq cm
1 square foot (sq ft)/144 sq in	= 929.03 sq cm
1 square yard (sq yd)/9 sq ft	= 8361.3 sq cm/0.8361 sq metre
1 acre/4840 sq yd	= 4046.9 sq metres/0.4047 ha
1 square mile/640 acres	= 259 ha/2.59 sq km

Volume

1 cubic centimetre (cu cm)/ 1000 cubic millimetres (cu mm)	= 0.0610 cu in
1 cubic decimetre (cu dm)/1000 cu cm	= 61.024 cu in/0.0353 cu ft
1 cubic metre/1000 cu dm	= 35.3146 cu ft/1.308 cu yd
1 cu cm	= 1 millilitre (ml)
1 cu dm	= 1 litre see **Capacity**
1 cubic inch (cu in)	= 16.3871 cu cm
1 cubic foot (cu ft)/1728 cu in	= 28.3168 cu cm/0·0283 cu metre
1 cubic yard (cu yd)/27 cu ft	= 0.7646 cu metre

Capacity

1 litre	= 1.7598 pt/0.8799 qt/0.22 gal
1 pint (pt)	= 0.568 litre
1 quart (qt)	= 1.137 litres
1 gallon (gal)	= 4.546 litres

Weight

1 gram (g)	= 0.035 oz
1 kilogram (kg)/1000 g	= 2.20 lb/35.2 oz
1 tonne/1000 kg	= 2204.6 lb/0.9842 ton
1 ounce (oz)	= 28.35 g
1 pound (lb)	= 0.4536 kg
1 ton	= 1016 kg

Pressure

1 gram per square metre ($g/metre^2$)	= 0.0292 oz/sq yd
1 gram per square centimetre (g/cm^2)	= 0.226 oz/sq in
1 kilogram per square centimetre (kg/cm^2)	= 14.226 lb/sq in
1 kilogram per square metre ($kg/metre^2$)	= 0.205 lb/sq ft
1 pound per square foot (lb/ft^2)	= 4.882 $kg/metre^2$
1 pound per square inch (lb/in^2)	= 703.07 $kg/metre^2$
1 ounce per square yard (oz/yd^2)	= 33.91 $g/metre^2$
1 ounce per square foot (oz/ft^2)	= 305.15 $g/metre^2$

Temperature

To convert °F to °C, subtract 32, then divide by 9 and multiply by 5
To convert °C to °F, divide by 5 and multiply by 9, then add 32

Phototypeset by Tradespools Limited, Frome, Somerset
Printed and bound by Artes Gráficas, Toledo, SA, Spain
D. L. TO: 1505 -1984